THE KING IS MY FATHER

A CHRISTIAN FANTASY TALE OF CREATION

A children's tale based on the fundamental
principles set forth by God, our creator.
cc.Feb. 2005, Helen Cage
Rev. 2007

MAE CAGE

authorHOUSE®

AuthorHouse™
1663 Liberty Drive
Bloomington, IN 47403
www.authorhouse.com
Phone: 833-262-8899

Published by AuthorHouse 09/01/2020

ISBN: 978-1-7283-7137-5 (sc)
ISBN: 978-1-7283-7138-2 (hc)
ISBN: 978-1-7283-7246-4 (e)

Library of Congress Control Number: 2020916748

Print information available on the last page.

Any people depicted in stock imagery provided by Getty Images are models, and such images are being used for illustrative purposes only. Certain stock imagery © Getty Images.

This book is printed on acid-free paper.

Because of the dynamic nature of the Internet, any web addresses or links contained in this book may have changed since publication and may no longer be valid. The views expressed in this work are solely those of the author and do not necessarily reflect the views of the publisher, and the publisher hereby disclaims any responsibility for them.

Scripture taken from the King James Version of the Bible.

Dedicated to all of the King's children

During the earthly life of every Christian child of God, there are attempts to entice and snare away the Christian from a loving God. This attempt will invariably be done by the only invention the ruler of this world has. The lie is used to deceive God's children in all areas of victory. God is truth and lies are meant to block the power of God's truth. But most importantly lies attack our belief and trust in what God the Father has promised for his children.

1 Thessalonians 5: 4-5

But ye brethren, are not in darkness, that that day should overtake you as a thief, 5) ye are all sons of light, and sons of the day; we are not of the night, nor of darkness

It is very important that every child of God understand and know that God has equipped his children with weapons to defeat these attempts, but just as important the Christian must understand that resistance will often bring on declared war by the enemy. Captives are taken in war. But One has already come to set the captives free. Bondage in any form can no longer be used to imprison God's children when we know and trust God's word.

The truth and the light will illuminate the way home, so that no matter how far we travel, the way is well lighted so long as we keep the truth in our hearts. Along the way there will be many to assist you and point out the way, but the word WHO became flesh is our compass.

Proverbs 22:6 tells us to "train up a child in the way he should go, and when he is old, he will not depart from it.

This is a tale for children of all ages with the hope that it will be of benefit in passing from the milk stage to the solid food stage (see Hebrews 5: 12-14)

Dedicated to all of the King's children

During the earthly life of every Christian child of God, there are attempts to entice and snare away the Christian from a loving God. This attempt will invariably be done by the only invention the ruler of this world has. The lie is used to deceive God's children in all areas of victory. God is truth and lies are meant to block the power of God's truth. But most importantly lies attack our belief and trust in what God the Father has promised for his children.

1 Thessalonians 5: 4-5

But ye brethren, are not in darkness, that that day should overtake you as a thief, 5) ye are all sons of light, and sons of the day; we are not of the night, nor of darkness

It is very important that every child of God understand and know that God has equipped his children with weapons to defeat these attempts, but just as important the Christian must understand that resistance will often bring on declared war by the enemy. Captives are taken in war. But One has already come to set the captives free. Bondage in any form can no longer be used to imprison God's children when we know and trust God's word.

The truth and the light will illuminate the way home, so that no matter how far we travel, the way is well lighted so long as we keep the truth in our hearts. Along the way there will be many to assist you and point out the way, but the word WHO became flesh is our compass.

Proverbs 22:6 tells us to "train up a child in the way he should go, and when he is old, he will not depart from it.

This is a tale for children of all ages with the hope that it will be of benefit in passing from the milk stage to the solid food stage (see Hebrews 5: 12-14)

May this tale take you on the journey of victory that Christians everywhere are traveling through our Lord Jesus Christ.

I did not and could not make this transition until I learned how much the Lord God Almighty loved me just as I am. Peace be unto you and yours.

Ephesians 3; 17-19

17) That Christ may dwell in your hearts by faith; that ye, being rooted and grounded in love,

18) May be able to comprehend, with all saints, what is the breadth, and length, and depth, and height,

19) And to know the love of Christ, which passes knowledge, ...

CONTENTS

Chapter 1   Christian in the Hog Trough 1

Chapter 2   Enter the King's Rest 27

Chapter 3   Who is the King? 43

Chapter 4   Lucre's Folly 57

Chapter 5   The Confrontation 81

Chapter 6   Lucre's Thief of the Children 111

Chapter 7   Preparing for Battle 129

Chapter 8   The Mountains Erupt 151

CHAPTER ONE

Christian in the Hog Trough

Prince Christian set among the pigs covered in the slimy mud and filth of the hog trough. The young boy's mind although strong, was struggling to concentrate on the decrees of his father. The decrees of his father give him and the other children authority to rule their domain; yet here they were slaves. The power to defeat all forces coming against the King's children was granted through knowledge and adherence to the King's decrees.

The boy Christian had uncanny ability to discern the intentions of those he came in contact with. Christian's eyes changed colors depending on his mood and what his inner spirit discerned within his environment. Right now his mind was locked in a fierce struggle to concentrate on the teachings of the Father. Anyone looking would see the color of his eyes had shifted from blue to black. There seem to be a storm raging from inside to outside, visible through the windows of his eyes.

Not having seen his father for many years did not prevent Christian from feeling him near. The struggle was to be one with the King.

The King, his father was ruler and creator of the entire universe. The King held court over all worlds and only he could establish universal law. The creator of all things, the King's vision was evident throughout the universe. It was Christian's right as the King's son to rule. Not just Christian's right, but the right of all the King's children who dared to accept the King's teachings as truth.

Much like his father, Christian was primarily a spirit being. The one major difference the King had given Christian and all his children was the earth suits they wore to encase the spirit beings. The King designed the earth suits from the very earth itself, thus making the children one with the earth they ruled. Every action of the King's had purpose,so it was with the earth suits. The children part of the earth, just as they were part of the King. So Christian and his many siblings were of two worlds, but to rule it was necessary to have an entrusted interest in the subject. The King was ruler over that which was entrusted to him, namely his children and the earth was entrusted to the children; giving them a legal right to rule the earth.

They were spirit like their father the King, and they were earth to be a part of the earth in which they were to rule.

The earth was to the children's to rule; however survival depended on staying connected to the Father through the spirit.

The only way to get into the spirit world while on earth was through the gateway of the mind. Christian's problem was, someone or something was trying to block that gateway to keep him separated from the King.

The mind created visions called imagination. Imagination was the way of seeing things in the mind before they were seen with the eyes. It allowed Christian to cause into existence events and material objects which were not previously there. To create Christian had only to see the object of his thought, and to speak directly to the intent of the object. That was how the King created all things. When the King wanted light he saw the sky in his thought and spoke to the intent of the sky, by stating "Let there be light." The result was the sky, which fulfilled the need for light among other needs. The used his thoughts to see all creation before he spoke with his words. So it was meant to be with the King's children.

Right now the struggle going on in Christian's mind was for that vital connection with his Father. Although his father wasn't there, it was as if Christian could feel the warm loving embrace he knew as a baby. But as always the embrace grew cold before he could completely absorb the warmth and strength that came with it. Christian could feel his Father, but his mind was being blocked from seeing his Father. It would be vital to master the ability of holding onto the embrace until he could see the love of his Father if he was to ever get back home.

Missing the love and friendship of friends back home, Christian thought of Joseph and Rudy, his companions. Together the group studied the writings of the King given out by the teachers. Included in the study was the practice of perfecting the usage of the sword called truth.

Practicing to wield the sword of truth was no easy task when placed in situations directly in conflict with truth. Once in the classroom the instructor had caused the images of strong wind and thunder to appear. The illusion was so powerful, although the boys knew they were still in the security of the classroom, it was difficult to remain clam. Only by slicing through the delusion by wielding the truth back and forth in their minds were they able to cut through the images. The sword of truth is double edged to cut what comes from the back as well as the attacks coming from the front, leaving a path of light. The sword cuts away all hindrances to the King. Deceit is that which does not match what the King said.

Deceit began to follow the children once they were separated from the King.

Master Eric keeper of the sword cautioned the boys to remember the sword was the connection to the King. Every part of the King is truth.

Under Master Eric's guidance the children wielded the sword of truth during practice to penetrate all areas of darkness. The sword of truth has a blade shapely entirely from light. A translucent light of blue. While it is true one can see through the blade, nothing can penetrate the blade. The blade was two edged, able to cut through darkness from all sides. When swung in a side to side motion, it not only cut a path, but a path of light. The path was broad for all who knew the truth to follow through. It brought much joy to see how easily truth produced light in darkness. The boys laughed in amazement as the darkness of deceit gave way to light. Those had been fun times, and he missed those times, but it had always been the children's responsibility for maintaining the knowledge gained during practice. It was no different now.

Now he was not home and tragedy had stuck. Although it was hard holding on to the knowledge entrenched in him as a child, the truth was still the same. And now he had failed one of the other children.

The way of life here revolved around events intended to produce anxiety to draw one's thoughts to consistent, present problems and over shadow the past teachings. The pressure hurled upon the imagination by such events prevented freedom of the mind to travel into the spirit realm where all power was stored until needed. Without lessons the knowledge became weak.

This is where we find Prince Christian. Struggling to free not only himself, but all the children. Adding to the problem Gayla was now being held and possibly tortured because of his attempts.

Thinking of the last encounter with Gayla produced a knot in his chest where his heart should be. During all the time here, nothing had ever hurt him as much as this.

Responsible for another was heavy burden, but a burden with many rewards. Christian could feel anew the love and admiration shown to him by Gayla as she thanked him for teaching of the King's love. "The awareness of a Father who loves me beyond understanding gives me hope for a future," Gayla stated as her eyes overflowed with tears. "Do not think me unhappy, dear Christian, she said upon seeing the alarm in his eyes. "These tears are for joy."

Recalling the encounter, Christian's heart was strengthening with joy remembering Gayla's joy. Christian felt his legs become weak. "I must not falter," he thought. "So much depends on getting the message to the children of the Father's love. Once the message was delivered it would depend on Emissary of the King to enlighten the mind of the children who were willing to receive.

Willingness, the key to freedom and success was within every child of the King. Willingness when fueled by desire released freedom to choose; freedom to believe one's own path was the right of each child. It was the children's decision to betray him which put Gayla in danger. The pain of betrayal from the family of the King's children, hurt more than any affliction Lucre could put upon him.

Still Christian held firm to the belief in his father's word. The word of the King was unchallengeable just as the King was, even here. There was a way to rescue Gayla and escape this life of drudgery. That way was the knowledge of the King's word. Knowledge and belief in the King's Word lead to practice. Practice would strengthen belief until belief produce the sword of truth. With the sword one was ready for battle. Christian's father had promised him, 'No weapon formed against you shall succeed. Your enemies shall fall for your sake.'

More than life itself, Christian needed to be connected to his father. "So long as you keep my word, you'll always have me," the King had promised and his father did not lie. Christian had to be united with his father to win this battle and save Gayla and the others.

The King and his word were one. To have the King's word was the same as having the King. Holding on to the decrees and promises of the King gave him strength to hope of returning to the beautiful, peaceful home created by the King.

Still it was difficult to follow the instructions of his father in the placed where he now resided. The King's teachings required him and all followers to reside in the highest sphere of the mind. "Think on that which is pure and righteous," the Father said. Constant pain and drudgery deflected one's mind to defeat. Thoughts of defeat gave way to believeth and believeth created reality. Thinking on what was pure, good and uplifting was the difficulty. But to enter into the King's reality, the mind must see what was good. The mind was like a third eye. Right thinking caused the mind's eye to see the possible. Currently this was no easy task. Circumstances of their current place had reduced them to living in pig sties and taking the leftovers of the one in control here.

The spirit realm was where the King's Kingdom existed. Everything originated from there and the only access while on earth was through the mind. He and all the King's children were intended to live in a state of complete control while inhabiting the earth realm. This was the purpose of the King. The body was for the earth, but the mind was to be forever joined to the King in the spirit realm, this allowed the children to see as the King saw.

The spirit realm was where all creation; past, present and future existed under the authority of the King. Time does not exist in the spirit realm. The King's children were called to rule the earth realm through the reality of the King. The King is the only reality there is. Everything else was make believeth; not real. It was dangerous for the King's children to engage in make believe.

For several months now a constant group had joined Christian in the secret meetings. In the past a few would attend, but eventually they stopped coming when the pressures of this place became overwhelming.

In this present location, the imagination of the children was taken over by deceitful earth thoughts planted by the evil Master Lucre. It was the evil Master Lucre who sought to separate the children from the creator and father; the King.

Lucre planted thoughts contrary to the King's decrees to hold the King's children in bondage on earth. Thoughts produced defeat and could actually produce a down trodden life. Planting the thoughts was the same as causing events to match the thoughts. This was possible because the children had the power to manifest whatever they imagined. So while he had no real power himself, Lucre held the children captive by their own thoughts. Causing day to day difficulties and applying constant pressure to control their thought process. The children's every thought was for survival by pleasing Lucre. Lucre had convinced them it was the only way they could live. In this way, Lucre kept them away from the King and from freedom.

Samuel and some of the other boys had briefly attended Christian's meetings. The boys were delighted to hear there was a way out of the stagnant, muddled, and constant drudgery of life and looked forward to the stolen moments of hope. Samuel had told Christian, "I always felt there was more to life than what I saw here and now I feel I may have a better life someday." The provision of hope provided by the King's words was affirmed by Samuel's statement to Christian.

It was at that time Lucre had his goons increase the boys' hours of labor; cutting down the time they had for themselves. With even less time, the boys had to stop coming to the meetings.

The only way to the King was to believe in His existence through thought, and Lucre was blocking the gateway to the spirit world by controlling their thoughts with circumstances involving earth life. Constant bombardment of negativity and seemingly impossible task keep the children in a state of depression. Lucre pushed the children beyond endurance with circumstances designed to overshadow the decrees of the King. Thoughts were influenced to hold the children in bondage to the very thing they were created to rule; the earth and everything in it.

Lifting the buckets with feed for the hogs, Christian preceded to head over to the hog trough. Eyes cast downward; Christian did not see the goon named Puton. Puton threw a large branch in Christian's path. Stumbling head forward the swill in the buckets fell inward covering Christian all over. Puton shouted with laughter and pigs bellowed in disruption.

The noise drew a crowd of goons and some children. Puton and the goons found the scene hilarious. Laughter mixed with spittle coming from mouths filled with broken green teeth could be heard vibrating throughout the area. The children shrink back, afraid to be seen in case they too were made objects of pain for the goon's enjoyment.

Christian lay face there, bracing himself for the pain sure to come with a beating by the goons. It wasn't long before he felt a boot to his bottom and heard Puton berate him for wasting the hog's food. Quickly Christian recalled words from the King within his mind assuring him joy would come after the pain. "For a little while suffering, then joy everlasting," Christian heard the words as though they were being spoken by the King, himself, that's because the command center for the children is the mind.

The goons used their clubs for the children's bodies, but the King's words protect the mind.

Circumstances created in the earth realm can have only temporary effect on the body, but the mind is able to access the spirit realm and actual change the effects on the body. Solutions created by the King from the beginning of time remaining infinitely accessible through spirit access. The King's solutions included everything that has existed, does exist, or will ever exist. Reality is the King's word and originates in the spirit realm, not on earth.

The biggest stumbling block for the children was their own ability to create false reality with the power given to them by the King. Powers intended to bestow ruler ship upon the children, no matter where they resided, was also the vehicle to destroy them. Lucre knew this and contrived to hide truth from those held in captivity. The thoughts of the children were being manipulated by circumstances fashioned out of lies to make a false reality. False hoods which when believed and acted upon became aberrant reality.

The true reality of Katerboro is that it is a suspended aberrant form of life created by the King for insurgent spirits who rebelled against the Kingdom. Katerboro was never meant to be a dwelling place for the King's children. Although the King has all control, the children must have knowledge of their granted authority to exert rule in the spirit world and beyond, including Katerboro. Katerboro is under the control of insurgent spirits lead by Lucre, because the children are not aware of their granted authority. All evil resides here. The children were being held captive here amid the evil because of the lack of knowledge. Evil was that which is in opposition to the King's law, including thoughts.

It had an actual location in the farthest region of the earth over ice covered mountains. To get there one had to travel over dangerous slippery ice covered mountain tops. A slip at any moment could cause one to fall into the never ending sleep.

Once there the land turned from ice to dry hot caverns and flat dirt covered lands. No vegetation suitable for the children's food or coverage from the heat grew here. The place was not meant to support the life forms of the children in body or spirit. This place was created for punishment to Lucre and his followers.

Once transported there total surrender to evil thoughts and actions was required to continue to exist. Total surrender was to become one of the insurgent spirits to be pitted against the King and separated from His love. The evil Master Lucre was leader here. It was never intended for the King's children. It was so much easier to get there, than to get from there.

The way for a child of the King to enter Katerboro was to fall prey to untruths. Believeth in untruths resulted in surrender of the children, making them slaves to deception. Lucre is the master over deception, thus making him master over those enslaved by deception. Once enslaved in Katerboro, they became children of the dark, estranged from the world of light.

Picking himself up from the ground, Christian looked for light in his present situation and found purpose. Christian had to help Gayla. This was his purpose.

With Lucre being the inventor of the lie and everything in Katerboro being based on lies; Katerboro is Lucre's Kingdom. When Lucre's lies controlled the minds of the children, they fall under the influence of Lucre. The resulting influence left the children in an unnatural state of defeat. Lies imposed on the minds of the children cause the children to see circumstances as they were contrived by the evil spirits of Katerboro, rather than as they actual were. Circumstances came to life first in the minds of the imprisoned inhabitants and then became a physical realty for those who believed them.

Therein lies the problem, the King's children are in dominion over all things by birthright. However in this one area, the children needed the authority of the King to do successful battle with Lucre. The children had been granted the King's authority, but what good is authority when one doesn't know he has it? Lucre's lies were designed to create doubt of the King's love for the children. Doubting His love, made it easy to doubt He had given them authority over all they see. Thus making the children powerless because of unbelief toward the King

. The dominion of the children is assured by the King's authority. Use of that authority must be ignited through knowledge and belief. The legitimacy of The authority is proven by the results. In this way the King gets glory.

Lucre was shred and knew to implant thoughts of doubt toward the King is the same as taking all power from His children. After years of captivity, the children lose their identity and the body dies, leaving their spirit captive in Katerboro. The only way to force them to stay in this place was to conceal who they are by deceit and hide their birthright.

To maintain separation from the King it is necessary to control of the thought process of the children. Blinding the children to their true identity renders them confused and powerless. Still the unlimited power was there within their minds. But operating without the benefit of light illuminated from the King's words; their thoughts created every dark image imaginable. Images of hate, fear, poverty, jealousy, envy were all products of a dark imagination at work. Images of their own making, based on lies tormented the children.

One could enter Katerboro at any time with little notice. The slow subtle process of being lured into the place could happen without warning if one was not alert. Daily doubt slowly drew the children into Katerboro. Following the decrees of the King was the only assurance of avoiding the horrible place. The intention of this place was to hold the children in bondage through an adulterated existence.

This is where we find Prince Christian. The children will be held captive in suspension for all eternity unless Christian can get them to recognize the power and authority given them through the King's decrees.

Christian's mission is to bring remembrance as to who they are and thus free the children to live as the King intended.

Time and time again his father had taught him the principles established for the Royal life of the King's children. These very principles governed everything concerning a child of the King. The King had never grown weary of teaching his beloved children. Now it was up to Christian to illuminate the light of the King and dispel the darkness from the mind of the children. A battle Christian grew stronger in every day since he was kidnapped and brought here to this strange foreign land. Yes the other children had been lured here by false promises, but Christian was forcibly taken; taken by Lucre, with the intent of using his mind to do evil. Christian was chosen because the one thing he knew for certain was the sure knowledge he was one with the Father because of the provisions made by the child. The child the father sent after the great betrayal.

Constant bombardment of thoughts of defeat was meant to block the presence of his Father. But the Father would never allow total separation between them. The sureness of this fact gives him confidence in his pursuit of the Kingdom of light. He knew he was assured of success and he, along with those he came for would succeed.

Often his mind would grow dim with the concerns of himself and the others here. At those times the instructions of the King grew vague and fuzzy. This is when he would withdraw and hide to meditate on the King's decrees. Meditation on the King's words brought not only comfort, but renewed strength as well.

Many earth years had passed since his capture. The purpose for his existence was being eradicated. Once he was a ruler and Prince, now everyday was filled with meaningless toil. The work here was not for joy and fulfillment, but designed for torture by the evil master, to reduce the children to mindless souls. The struggle for survival only ended each day suspended in agony. Daily life consisted of toiling to the commands of a master unable to give peace or life. There was no joy in Katerboro.

Christian held back the tears as the memory of the morning came rushing into his mind. Grabbing the pail of scraps and fat he busied himself feeding the hogs. Guilt and shame at having been captured would often seize his mind in an attempt to overtake him. Deep inside Christian knew it was not his fault he was captured, but the guilt came to break his spirit. Now added to that was the blame he felt for Gayla's current punishment.

With no time for tears and too late to look to the past, he busied himself with the heavy burden of his work. If he was caught not working, the man-beaters would converge upon him with sticks and fist. Man-beaters were only one group of Lucre's many followers. Each group craved to be more furious than the others. To receive praise from Lucre, pain needed to be inflicted upon the children and they all wanted praise from their master.

Still the pain of the morning events was having a weakening effect upon his mind. The effect shut out the light of the mind, resulting in blindness to the King's words. He could not allow his body to become weak also. It was vital to keep moving. Otherwise the man-beaters would descend upon him and he needed to find Gayla.

Gayla a young girl of thirteen was Christian's closest confident in this place. She above all, had seemed to understand when he recalled his father's words for the children to hear. This alone was reason enough to save the girl. Gayla was one of the few with "ears to hear" and the mind's eye capable of seeing the world he described. That world had been forgotten by most of the child inhabitants of Katerboro. Gayla could become a voice to speak of the King to others and thereby help to free the children.

Gayla had suffered much abuse by the goons, still her spirit remain strong. Due to the possession of the mind by Lucre, the spirit world of the King was totally beyond the children's ability to imagine; but she above all had the capabilities to see beyond their present circumstances. Perhaps it was because of the suffering, she was willing to believe. Having lost all, why not believe?

The original purpose of the earth world created by the King for His beloved children had been expunged from sightless minds. Christian sought to give sight of that purpose and the plans his father had for those he created to rule. Gayla understood. Now she was being torture because of him.

The memory of his father's love came flooding into Christian's heart. The intensity of the memory caused Christian's knees to buckle and he dropped the pail as he fell to the ground. The slime from the bucket spilled over Christian's body and immediately the hogs were eating and slurping away at the young boy. Always the hogs seem to be present.

Just for a moment the boy just wanted to give in to hopelessness and succumb to the greedy hogs. The struggle seems so great and his emotions were weakening due to Gayla's dilemma. The huge brown eyes were now clouded to black, moist with tears and emotion. "Oh, if only he can find strength to get up from beneath the pigs."

At the point of letting go, a surge of strength rose up inside the young boy. Despite the heartache inside him, Christian thrust out his arms to cast off the fiendish hogs. Emotions were not going to control him; he would control what he felt with his thoughts. "I have the ability to bring the King's promise of victory within my control. It is my right as the King's son," Christian spoke aloud.

The sounds of squealing is loud as Christian picked up hogs twice his size and hurled them out the opening on the side of the hog trough. The helpless anger he felt at Gayla being snatched was used as energy to fight off the hungry hogs. Hogs made cruel with Lucre's evilness. Christen found the thing which had almost weaken him to the point of defeat could be used as a tool for strength.

Just as quickly as he had fallen, Christian regained his composure and picked up the bucket. At that moment a man-beater passed and peered into the hog trough, but all was calm. Christian had avoided a beating. Once again the words of his father echoed in his head, "I will cause all things to work for your good and I will never abandon you, my son."

Looking at the blood running down his arm from the bite of a hog he felt strength from overcoming the fall and avoiding further trouble. It was a small victory, but every victory was needed. Had he still been on the ground when the man-beater came by, he would surely have been beaten and possibly killed

Christian turned his thoughts back to Gayla. Often just as evening was dawning, Christian and a group of seven or eight children would sneak away to the back of the hog trough. Here Christian would tell of the land where their father ruled. Christian tried to make the others see with his words all the beauty and enchantment of his father's kingdom. It was no easy task and the hardest part was to convince the others that not only was the King his father, but he was also their father. The children had no memory of the King. They lived a state of defeat, surpassed only by total death of the spirit.

It was like explaining the beautiful colors of a flower to someone who lives only in a world of black and white with no perception of colors or shapes. Still he had to try and convey the unconditional love and peace that was theirs by birthright. They would have to be able to see it to believe it and belief was key to obtaining it.

The kingdom of their father was in sharp contrast to this dark, cold world where they now lived in. Here they were slaves. Forced to toil and labor for the pleasure of evil beings whose only thought was to cause defeat to the children of the King, they were of less value than the hogs. Just as the thought occurred to Christian, he heard the scream of Chen as a goon kicked him.

In his father's kingdom, they were rulers govern by the declarations of the King. Declarations which established the principles for the continuation of the world as the King created it until time indefinite. The wish of the

King was for all his children to have success and strength throughout all eternity, while each of their spirits remained joined to the King.

The King's principles were the foundation of law and his principles are founded entirely on his truths. "The Father's spiritual truths are reality and everything else is a lie. The Father's truth is the children's truth and no amount of lies could ever change that," Christian chanted these words before and after each gathering he conducted. Sooner or later he believed the words would reach them and they would grasp the truth of what he said.

It was because of the King's teachings; Christian knew truth was unchangeable, regardless where one resided. Everything in this place operated on lies to blind the children. The results of this life were only a fabricated existence created by deceit to further the desires of the evil one who would be master.

Waiting for the goon to pass Christian sneaked over to Chen to encourage the boy with words of the Father. Suffering is only for a little while; you shall have peace after a while." Chen not knowing what peace was only looked at Christian in pain.

Chen was often picked on by some of the other children. That was an another product of this place. Pain and defeat caused hurting children to attempt to elevate themselves by stomping on those seen as weak.

Christian was determined to open the minds of the children to the truth that would give them freedom from this slavery they now existed in. "The truth is, we are of Royal blood and rulers over all things seen and unseen, second only to our father the King. Truth is what will give us our freedom. If you can believe the truth as given by the King, no one will ever be able to enslave you again," said Christian at the secret meetings. Always he searched for a sign of acceptance while speaking. The faces of those around remain fixed and indifferent until last night's meeting had produce results at last.

Every child of the King was born with the truth within him, but the life they lived was intended to force the truth out of them by a piling on lies. Truth was written in the declarations of the King, but there was no written word here. Lucre forbids books of the King. The King who knew all things had stated, "By the spoken word one shall be justified and by the spoken word one shall be condemned." Christian felt the responsibility to restore the truth back to the minds of the children by speaking the King's declarations. Lucre used words to condemn the children. Christian had to continue to find opportunity to speak the King's words to the children. It was the only way the children would hear the declarations and thus regain the power to free themselves of their current slavery. Christian reminded himself, "How are they to know the truth unless they hear the truth?"

At an early age, Christian had experienced the proven power of words when spoken in truth. Power was manifested by words when spoken from the mouth of a King's child. It had been a shadowy morning and several children were teasing Christian. Normally Christian turned a deft ear to the teasing of the other children, but this day the spirit of discernment was strong on the boy. Looking at one child in particular, a boy called Horatio, the young boy could see within the other child to the falseness hidden there. Horatio was teasing Christian for things out of his control, when he himself was a liar.

Against the King's admonition, Christian let anger in for a moment and began chiding the boy for the lies he was spreading. Immediately a curse landed on the boy and he became agitated and began to cry in pain. Christian at first was astonished at the power of his spoken word. When spoken with confidence and expectation, his words had produced an outcome aligned with the truth of the words. Then he became ashamed at using his power so casually. He was moved to remorse because the words were not spoken out of love. Horatio had given consent for the curse to be effective by bullying Christian. Horatio's actions placed him outside the protection form curses. Had Horatio not been offensive, the curse would not have affected him. Still Christian knew he should have been forgiving. Did not the King expect forgiveness?

Apologetic and canceling the words of damnation spoken over Horatio, Christian knew he could never use his gift in such a frivolous way again. Christian willingly gave forgiveness to the one who had agitated him and he sought forgiveness for himself. He vowed to avoid those who could tempt him to speak without given thought to the outcome of spoken words. From that moment he knew first hand he was responsible for the power unleased by his speech. Christian learned a valuable lesson. The overabundance of wrong actions and thoughts can twist the purpose of speech and yoke one to evil.

It was for this reason Christian had conviction to start the meetings. Tucked away in the dark, damp corner of the pig trough, the meetings were intended to rouse the King's word inside the children and give them liberty to speak as the King had declared. Christian began the lecture by stating, "Each of you have a portion of the King living inside of you. That portion is in the form of the King's Spirit. The King has taken care to ensure nothing will ever separate his children from him by putting His Spirit inside each child. The Spirit of the King gives power to your spoken words when aligned to the Kings thoughts."

"This was done with the first created man, our ancestor and has been passed through birth to each new child. Each time a child is formed the Spirit divides and inserts into the new baby. Because the King is unlimited so is His Spirit, making division possible no matter how many children are born. With the inserted Spirit, power is given to the King's children. However because of a state of lawlessness which was not your fault, that Spirit is asleep inside you at this moment." The Spirit thrives where there is love and goodness among the children.

"To awaken the Spirit of the King and all the power it has requires your spoken word to mimic the King's thoughts. It requires your spoken declaration of agreement with the King. Everything of beauty ever made was made by this Spirit through words spoken by the King. You are children of the King and like the King you must activate the Spirit's power through words."

"The Spirit is love and has all power to cause all things to work for the benefit of the King's purpose. The King's purpose is for the good of His children at all times, even here." After finishing the last word, Christian looked around the small space searching for some sign of understanding. He had not found that recognition until last night. Last night Gayla had comprehended the words he spoke. Gayla had heard the King's Spirit and proven all truth can only be revealed by the Spirit.

The harsh circumstances of life in this hard place had captured the awareness of the children, holding them in bondage to fear and hopelessness. Now the Spirit, the very power to free them, was lying dominant, unheard and unused. Christian knew the realization of truth was the key to getting the children to believe, and belief was the only way to arouse the Spirit.

In order for belief to occur it was necessary for the child to first hear the truth. One thing depended on the other. It was the process of the principle of faith as designed by the King. Once a child heard and recognized the truth, the Spirit inside them would cause them to speak truth unleashing power to accomplish that which was spoken. Recognition was the key. Without recognition the lies would continue to blind each child. But each child had to recognize truth for himself.

Truth spoken out of the mouth of the King's children would unleash all the power needed for the children's freedom from all danger. The children had to be awakened from their slumber before they perished into eternal darkness. All these thoughts twirled in the mind of Christian impressing the importance of the young man's mission.

On the night of the fourth meeting as always, Christian had started the meeting with the lecture of the Spirit. To end Christian would always encourage the children to express gratitude to the King for His love. Expressing feelings of joy was done to give the children hope they could carry with them after the meeting as well as to open their minds to goodness. "If he could get them to know the King's love under these conditions, they would have no trouble believing in a King of goodness," he reasoned within his mind. "Then perhaps they could envision the beautiful Kingdom which was their home. Only with love could they experience the King and all that he had for them." Instead of focusing on the bad conditions they were forced to live under, Christian spoke words of gratitude to the unseen father. None of the children could find anything to be thankful for so they only watched.

This went on for about ten minutes. The other children looked on wanting to experience this imaginary King but unable to believe in His existence. Most only came as a diversion from the drudgery of their life. Then suddenly Gayla's voice could be heard with Christian's voice. At first the girl's voice was so low the words were inaudible then gradually the sound grew louder until the words of love and trust were clearly understood. "Great King we thank you for love and knowledge of your greatness."

Gayla was expressing love for a King she did not know. The others looked on in shock, watching in amazement as the girl's face appeared to glow. Then she not only spoke with lightness, but she begins to dance with abandonment as though she was taken over by another life. Everyone knew the trouble Gayla experienced daily. How could she experience feelings of joy?

Chen, an eleven-year-old boy with deep searching eyes and curly brown hair looked at Christian with puzzlement in his eyes. When Chen was troubled or confused, the iris of his eyes became dark brown. Right now Christian could see the boy's eyes were blazing with sparks. "What have you done to her?" Chen asks Christian. "You've enchanted her with magic?

Chen had been born here in the land of Katabareo, his mother being one of the early ones ensnared by the promise of greatness made by Lucre.

Like the other children, once she was lured here she was force to obey him or pay a high price for not accepting his way. Unfortunately for her and the others like her they took the easier way. As a result they were beaten down.

Chen never knew his father so he could not imagine this father Christian spoke of or any father for that matter. But then Chen had no comprehension of what love was either. His mother was always working to please Lucre and thus keep herself and Chen alive. Having never known anything different, Chen thought life was supposed to be hard and miserable and then one day you would go to sleep and never wake up. Sometimes Lucre was responsible for someone falling asleep, but no one dared say so aloud.

Chen had first been put to work in the hog tough at age four, and then when he grew taller at age seven, he was selected to help the adult workers. Anyone over four feet tall was subjected to work. Age didn't matter, only the ability to work and perform the needed task. Children were not separated from the adults in the work. Everyone shared in the hardship of Katerboro except Lucre and his gang. But Chen and the others at the meeting did have something to be grateful for. As of this moment they had not been sent to work the mines. No one ever came back from the mine.

Christian had been helping to build the barns for over four years now. Being tall and lean he did as much work as many of the men. Health and strength was not long-drawn-out. It was this way with both boys and girls of size. You had to grow up fast in Lucre's dwelling place.

Lucre greatest joy was ensnaring and trapping the children of the King. Always he created discontent by dangling unanswered desires with a promise of achieving the desired thing his way. Whether it was unrequited love or delayed dreams, Lucre fooled the children into thinking that with his help they could achieved whatever they sought. It was only after they had joined him did they realize he had tricked them.

Lucre enjoyed being cruel to everyone; even the animals were subject to his cruelty. But the most fun was in tricking the children. Every time he succeeded in getting one of them to follow him, he felt a personal victory over the King. Each time he tricked one of the children, he felt he had personally wounded the King. The look on Lucre's face when he hurt someone was the only reference Chen had for power. It was this image that motivated his words now.

"How do we defeat Lucre? We don't have magic powers to conjure up spells." Christian replied, "I'm trying to make you understand there is no magic. It's all just part of Lucre's lies."

"You're crazy boy! I saw Lucre use a spell to afflict Oscar with great spots which turned into lumps on his back," Chen stated. "No Chen. Lucre told you and Oscar that he would cause the spots and lumps. Your mind then conceived the things he spoke of. He didn't do it. There was no magic. You and Oscar created the spots and lumps through your imagination. I'm trying to give you the true picture your mind was created for. A picture of health and a good life. Why is it easier for you to believe Lucre rather the truth of the King's word? The King said you have power over all evil. Can't you see yourself with that power?" The King gave the ability for you to exercise power through the child of long ago.

But all Chen saw was Gayla dancing around in what appeared to be joy. Surely Christian had learned Lucre's tricks and was now beguiling his friend. He wanted to believe the things Christian spoke of, but it was beyond anything he could imagine.

He made the choice to accept the reality of what he knew rather than to accept Christian's words. After all it didn't matter what joy was or if what Gayla was showing was real because he was sure joy did not belong in a place like this. Even if joy was real it couldn't last here.

Looking at Christian now, Chen felt certain that this time Christian had gone too far. It was all they could do to avoid Lucre and his evil band, now they would have to be on watch for tricks from Christian. Sure he was always talking about the King who was suppose to be a Father to everyone, but now he was trying to convince them to be thankful and speak words of gratitude to an unseen King. Worst of all Gayla was now caught up in this nonsense. Chen was sure the girl would only get hurt.

Christian seeing the confusion on the Chen's face, felt over whelmed with love for the older boy. "Chen the Father never intended life to be as you have known it. It is a good thing to work and to see your hands achieve good. No matter how dirty or hard the work, you can have the feeling of accomplishing good.

Train your mind to control your feelings through faith in the King's Word and you can control the world around you. You can experience joy in the work given you without accepting this way of life. Discontentment will serve to harden you, but hope will keep you alive. You must be able to see your way out of here"

One of Chen's jobs was to help maintain the silos. The silos were kept full of rotten food and other foul smelling things for the pigs. Chen would let enough silage out at intervals during the day. Christian and others like him would then fill buckets to take the swill to the hogs. If left to get the slop for themselves, the hogs would eat until they burst. This way the hogs were always well feed but were not killed until Lucre needed them. Lucre liked the hogs to be fat.

Helping to build and maintain the barns meant long hot days and maintaining the silos meant walking for miles. The trenches cover miles of land because of the many hogs. Lucre loved hogs. Hogs were filthy, nasty animals, always pushing and greedy. Lucre seems to think they were the best things here. Often by the end of the day, Chen had walked so far checking trenches that by night fall he was to far away to return to his dingy sleeping quarters. On these nights he would just curl up in the trench to sleep. The rotted meat kept him warm all night. Even though the days were always hot, the nights were usually cold.

"Work is one the many gifts the Father has given to his children. Through work we experience creation as well as production. Did you know that the Father created all of us? Through work we can give to others just as the father gave to us. The greatest joy you will ever feel comes from giving to others. We will search for the good in our situation until the time arrives to fight. In this way we build strength."

Christian reached out to take the older boy's hand, "Chen it seems impossible the things I say to you, but if you can just start to believe, everything will become clear to you. The world you see around you is a lie and the only way you will see your true world is to believe the Father's word."

Chen stood five feet, six inches in height. His hands were large and callus from years of hard work. Still it was evident Chen was little boy. The innocence of his years was in his mannerism and the way he stared you straight in the eye. Too innocent to turn away or avert eye contact, Chen wanted for an answer.

The shade of Chen's skin was not easily distinguishable, due to years of exposure to harsh elements and too much dirt to ever wash away with one washing. Chen's skin could be of the lightest pallor or perhaps a dark pigment but the one sure thing, which could not be mistaken, was the dullness in his eyes. Eyes empty of knowledge and understanding, void of all feeling other than hurt and pain.

The hurt and the pain were as much a part of Chen's eyes as hunger was a constant companion to his stomach. The only way the hurt, the pain or the hunger could leave would be if Chen were dead and even then perhaps they would stay. Christian placed Chen's hand over his own heart. "Here is where you will feel the love of the Father, just believe the Father's words and he will give you life without pain. He will show you joy. Chen snatched his hand away and wiped it on his dirty pant leg as though to wipe away the hog's filth. Without realizing what it was he felt, Chen sought to wipe away the flicker of hope he felt.

"Christian you fill your head with worthless dreams which will only get you into trouble. Not only that but you try to convince the rest of us that your worthless dreams are truth. We know nothing of this thing you call joy. We work because if we don't Lucre will torture us, we don't work to help others but to stay alive in this miserable place. Even though sleep may be better than this, we don't know, so we do what it takes to hold onto what we do know. How can you expect us believe something we know nothing of? If this world we live in is a lie as you said, at lest we know this lie, we don't know your truth or your King's truth. Christian we have no time to dream. You'll get Gayla hurt if she starts to believe your dreams."

Immediately Christian remembered his Father saying, "My people perish because of lack of vision." Chen continued on, "Dreams are for Lucre and those in his inner circle, not for you, me and the others. We can only do that which Lucre requires of us and he does not require us to dream. You lived in there with him when he first stole you and brought you here. I was young, but I remember the beautiful young baby he brought here for all of us to worship. But you persisted in remembering your Father and talking about his kingdom now look at you. You're here among the pigs with the rest of us trying to talk us into your dream world. You were too dumb to stay in the comfort of the house, but you want us to believe that you can show us a better way of life. Lucre decides your fate here, not your Father, even if he is a King!"

With that Chen stomped away through the mud. For one brief moment, he had felt something inside when Christian had placed his hand over his heart. The feeling although brief had frightened him; it was such a strange funny feeling.

That had been last evening. Now this morning a group of Lucre's burley men had come for Gayla. Gayla was so beautiful even when caked in mud. Dazzling hazel eyes illuminated her bronze skin even with the mud caked on.

Last evening when Chen stomped off in anger, Gayla had been quick to come to Christian's side. Looking into Christian's eyes, Gayla whispered "I believe." Gayla didn't understand why, but something about the stories told by Christian was very real to her. It was as though the stories reminded her of a life from long ago. But of course that was ridiculous, because she had spent her entire life here. Still she felt the truth of the words spoken about his father. Something had been awaken inside her.

Much later Gayla would understand the spirit of the King planted inside her was responsible for this feeling. But at that moment she responded to a need to give comfort. "It felt good to give comfort," she thought. "Perhaps the King had created her that way?" She didn't know, but at this moment she long to comfort the troubled young boy before her.

Looking deeply into Christian eyes she affirmed the trust shared between the two without speaking to him. "Come," she called to everyone, "we had better get back to work before we're missed." As Christian watched the tall slim figure of Gayla lead the other children away, he had felt hope.

Christian's Father had always stressed the importance of planting a seed for what you expected to grow. The seed of truth had found a resting place in Gayla and Christian was overjoyed. Surely the seed would grow and sprout to become a vine winding and twisting among all the children here. This thought produced a funny picture in his mind and Christian began to laugh inside. It felt good to laugh. Just as the seed of truth had given Gayla a moment of freedom, he was sure it would produce more fruit. Then there would be freedom for all, freedom from this life of bondage. Gayla had known freedom briefly.

That was last night and Christian had fallen asleep dreaming he was setting at his father's feet listening to the soothing voice of love. The King's voice always gave such peace even in a dream.

Now morning was here.

CHAPTER TWO

Enter the Kings Rest

That had been last night. With morning the evil men came. Dark and boisterous with hairy arms the size of large hams, the men screamed shouts of excitement and with eagerness. They wanted Gayla.

The men were part of Lucre's fighting team. For sport Lucre had teams that competed for prizes. The winner earned the right to pick one of the children to use for their pleasure. The fights served several purposes. The most important was that it kept the fiends away from the children until a designated time. Lucre's fiends were mean and angry. They could be seen gnawing and gnashing their teeth on unseen objects at all times of day or night. The children were their favorite targets. They took great pleasure in torturing the stolen children. If not restrained they would destroy the children before Lucre had time to use them in his war with the King. Lucre needed the children. They were his only tool to fight the King with. He desired to cause the children to suffer in hopes they would kill themselves. Lucre relied on his ability to lie to cause suffering in the children.

The only way Lucre could control how many children were tortured was to stage the fights with the children as prizes. The winning team was allowed to pick one of the children for their pleasure. Everyone knew that whoever was picked never came back. This morning Gayla was the chosen prize.

Suddenly the dark damp atmosphere of this place felt twice as heavy to Christian. The high dark mountains looked even more terrifying than before. The bright red fire shooting from the tops of the mountains appeared to be more luminous. The fire burned constantly. Often there were rumbles in the ground and the flames would leap even higher. The mountains themselves were covered in black soot and ash. The soot and ash covered the entire village, including the people. Lucre's dwelling was the largest in the village. The village was approximately 96 kilometers in diameter. Of this space all 96 kilometers was covered in slimy black ash. The ash was not dry but contained a substance which allowed the ash to stick to everything it touched. No one knew the way into or out of the village except Lure.

The ash covered Lucre's dwelling which was a large cave set into one the mountains. Many children worked inside the dwelling to provide comfort for Lucre and his fiends and often-horrible screams could be heard coming from his dwelling. For this reason no one wanted to venture near the place unless forced to come near.

Now the men were roaming the grounds looking for Gayla to take her there. Christian knew that he could not let the emotion of fear take over his heart. Carrying on the act of feeding the hogs was causing him to become dizzy. Where was she? Was she in hiding? Hadn't his Father warned him, that fear would render him powerless? There were so many thoughts running around in his head. No, he had to cast off the impeding feeling of fear creeping upon him.

Then before he could get past the fear, weakness in his knees forced Christian to drop to the ground for a second time that morning. Recalling Chen's agitation at last night's meeting, an ugly image flashed before Christian's eyes. Could Chen be the cause of Gayla being taken? Would he go so far just to prove Christian wrong? No, Chen would not allow Gayla to be taken. Clutching at his chest Christian forced air into his lungs and tried to think clearly.

This was the work of the Pythons. The Pythons were a part of Lucre's fiends. Spirits of divination, they are invisible to earthly eyes but made their home in dark worlds such as Katerboro. The Pythons main function was to whisper words of betrayal about those depending on others or mixing in social gatherings. They were able to foretell the negative outcome by judging the body language of the children. They were masters at judging the children.

At work, at play any time the children gathered together the Pythons were there whispering negative thoughts. The whispers were a way of planting seeds of destruction into the minds of the children and of course the children had no knowledge of the King's decree "forbidding them to be easily offended." In this way Lucre could be sure of division among the children. Lucre knew the power generated when the children came together in agreement. It gave Lucre a headache just to think of what would happen if they join together. "It was vital to cause separation among the children," Lucre instructed the Pythons.

Christian knew focusing on his environment would bring about destructive thinking. Focusing on his troubles would allow the Pythons easy access to his imagination and cause his speech to be treacherous and generate a harvest of bad circumstances from the negative seeds.

"Likewise pain and hopelessness are impostors seeking to gain entry into my heart through the words of the Pythons. Depression will result from those two seeds and I'll be useless to Gayla. No Lucre knows the law of seed time and harvest time. The Pythons are at work here turning me against the ones I must help," Christian said aloud.

He spoke the words aloud remembering the King's instructions, "Resist evil and it will flee." "Might as well let the Pythons know the game was over so they would leave," he said. Then speaking directly to the unseen demons he said, "Be gone in the name of the highest."

Christian's goal was to plant the seed of the King's Word. But right now fear for Gayla was absorbing his entire thinking process. Fear was a persistent intruder. Constantly looking for an entry into the mind and heart, fear thrived here in this dark damp place. It was always ready to lunge upon you. But hadn't his father warned him that fear would cause the imagination to malfunction? That would mean more negative seed coming from his imagination.

"I must remember the King's instructions. The King instructed me that I was created from the spirit world and that my imagination was the gateway into that world. My imagination will cause words to form needed to empower my imagination." An imagination gone wild would cause entry into the dark area of the spirit world. An imagination gone wild would cause words to form giving power to evil spirits. He must clear his head of frightful thoughts and think of his father.

Quickly Christian began to speak to himself and to tell himself that Gala would be O.K. He could hear his father telling him, "Speak to your mountain and cause it to move." But it would not be enough just to mutter any words; he had to speak his father's words. Only his father's words carried the authority to effect change. The power was unleashed when the King's words were spoken in belief of the authority they carried. They carried the King's authority.

"Keep the King's Word at all times," Christian repeated over and over. Hadn't his father told him, "As you think, so it will go with you." A man can only be as great as his smallest thought." He heard his father say, "Fear not for I am with you." Then it was brought to his thoughts that "Many are the afflictions of the virtuous: but the King is able to deliver all from trouble." Reflecting on these words, Christian remembered all the times he was faced with trouble when he tried to obey the King. Troubles always seem to go hand in hand with obedience. This would be a new encounter for Gayla, but one that would be repeated often if she continued to believe.

Concentrating on his Father's words, he began to talk with his Father. Although he didn't understand or know how it happened, he never doubted the King would hear him when they spoke together. Feeling the unseen King, Christian requested strength for Gayla. Slowly the anger and bad thoughts toward Chen started to lessen the dominance they had over him with. As a man he must never be dominated by anything. He was to be the dominator over all things. This was the truth he must convey to the children.

Katerboro bore all the ill effects of Lucre. Many years ago Lucre had cause the King's children to begin a descent into darkness by causing them to imagine evil against their brothers and sisters. As part of his training, the King had warned him to take heed of the enemy's ways.

Knowing that Lucre could not create, Christian knew that he would use the same tricks over and over. The words he spoke gave strength to his heart and made him feel close to the King. It was something he had learned long ago, talking to his Father assured him the King was near. Christian continued to tell his Father of Gala's troubles just as though his Father stood before him. Slowly the feeling of being powerless was being pushed away by a strange peace. Although he still did not know what to do, the boy had confidence he would receive direction from the one who knew the end of all things.

Continuing with his work, Christian found comfort in feeling his Father close by; still his heart felt such pain. Gala, the one who believed without ever seeing his Father; this was the one taken to be an object of cruelty. Although he knew she would be O.K., Christian also knew that she would suffer many pains. Thinking this thought, he once again ask his Father to strengthen the young girl so that she would not give in to pain that was ahead.

Several hours had passed since he first learned that Lucre's fiends were searching for Gala. During this time the children had continued to work as usual. No one would dare to stop or to show concern. To care about the other children was not encouraged and would only cause the concerned party to share in the punishment.

Knowing this outcome fought down feelings of fear and panic. He was not afraid to face punishment, but he did not want to run the risk of being placed in shackles. To be shackled would only complicate matters. He needed to be able to go to Gayla. However it wasn't long before Chen and some of the other trackers came by. Trackers were the workers who filled the silos.

Upon seeing the accusation in Chen's eye, Christian knew that Chen had not played a part in Gayla being chosen. As if to confirm this thought, at that moment there was a scream like nothing ever heard before. Chen and Christian locked eyes; each knowing what the scream meant. Gayla had been found.

Not thinking of consequences Christian ran to where the scream came from. Two of the ghoulish fiends had Gayla, one by each arm. Even from this distance there was no mistaken the terror on the girl's face. One phrase resounded in Christian's mind. "Hasten unto the throne." Christian knew he must seek out his father alone. He could not win this battle on his own.

Turning back the way he had come from Christian ran for his secret place. Chen and the others saw Christian's rapid retreat. The sneer on Chen's face could be heard in the words he called to the back of the fleeing boy, "I guess we know what you believe now!" But nothing compared to the heart wrenching pain Gayla felt when she saw Christian turn and run. The sight left her weak and she stopped struggling against the fiends.

Christian knew that his father heard every word he spoke and most of all; Christian knew that his Father spoke back. Many things had been revealed to him by the inner voice he had come to recognize as his father. He needed instructions on what to do.

During the early stages of his captivity, Christian had become aware of the quiet voice. The first time he heard the voice, he had almost missed it. It had been a day when all his emotions were wrapped up in loneliness and the pain of being away from the King's Kingdom. He felt so miserable. His head was filled sad and negative thoughts. Amid all the negative thoughts running around in Christian's head, there had been a very small voice crying out to him.

Christian didn't know how long the voice had been crying out to him before he finally heard it. However once he heard the voice, Christian was certain the voice had been there all along. The voice comforted the lonely little boy and gave him peace. At the point when peace came; Christian could clearly hear the words spoken by the voice, words of strength, comfort and assurance.

It had taken much concentration and meditation for Christian to learn how to keep the voice at all times, but now it was impossible to separate from the voice. Though sometimes it was quiet, it was there at all times.

The voice was needed for war. It was the voice of a general giving strategic command during battle. It was the voice of soothing comfort during times of crisis. It was the sound of love during loneliness. It was the King speaking to His child.

Christian was running to be alone with the voice now. Skirting the outer edges of the encampment, Christian avoided the battalion of the grotesque evil beings Lucre set guard over the valley at all times. There seem to be a protective covering shielding him from the eyes of all who would harm him. It was important to receive guidance and direction at this time of trouble. He must never attempt to fight without a battle plan from the King. Gayla's life depended on it and to fight without the King would mean certain defeat.

There was no doubt in the boy's mind, he knew the King would not only comfort him, but he would also tell him what to do. The King would leave nothing to chance; he would provide deliverance as well as peace for Gayla. It was this confidence that encouraged the boy's feet with the swiftness of a gazelle to his secret place to talk with the King.

Any time Christian gave in to feeling sorry for himself or let anger at his situation overtake his thoughts; the voice became very weak and sometimes silent. All these things had not been learned overnight, but Christian had finally understood the importance of being in control of his emotions. Dominance was his rightful position and the only position that would assure his victory. That was the law of the King.

Christian knelt before the huge boulder that was his makeshift Altar in his secret meeting place to be with the King. In the Kingdom there were Altar's of gold to meet with the King. Here this served as his Altar; an unmovable rock. An Altar was a place of transformation.

Having reached his Altar, he let go of all his defenses and surrendered his feelings to the King. Allowing himself to feel fear and weakness, the boy gave all to the King. The release of tears reduced the young boy to putty. This was the place of change. There was no need to hold anything back. Here he could not only show his weakness; but he would leave all frailties here at this Alter. Trading his weakness for strength from the King, Christian the boy ceased to be and was transformed by the power of the King's spirit joining with his spirit. The quiet voice inside said, "Through your weakness I can show my strength. Never be afraid to come to me Christian my son."

With this transformation the decree of the King went into effect "No weapon formed against him could succeed." It was this conversion in the children that Lucre feared. All his lies and deceit was meant to keep them bond in fear and anxiety so they would never be able to give all to the King. Lucre knew that once a child of the King reaches the point he or she is able to surrender all fear and panic into the King's hand; at that point the child enters the King's rest. The King's rest gives total freedom from anxiety and the King goes to work on behalf of His child. Victory is for sure. On this day Christian entered into the rest of the King and confidence swelled to overflow in the boy's thoughts. The preparation was set for the battle which was to come.

It was the inner voice that had first alerted Christian to Lucre's true nature. This was later confirmed with stories told by elders. The elder not knowing how to enter into the rest of the King would be full of despair and hopelessness. Hoping to find rest from all his fears in the forbidden drank found in Lucre's house, he would steal the drink from the house.

Although the elder thought he had acted to steal the drink, the guards were fully aware of the elder's actions and would allow the elder to drink the poisonous liquid until all reasonable thought was gone. The guards allowed this to make merriment. But only the fiendish guards were laughing. Often after drinking the liquid the elders would began to cry and mummer about the condition of life in Katerboro. This was a source of much joy for the guards. The complaints of the elder was a signal to the fiends the elder was in a state of defeat. The brutal fiends enjoyed seeing the elders in a state of self pity and for hours they would urge the elder to wail in despair.

As soon as the guards tired of the game the elder would be kicked out into the yard or depending on which guard was on duty, sometimes the elder was led into the pen with the dogs. If the elder was lead drunken into the pen with the dogs, their cry could be heard all over the camp. Long after the cry was over, the laughter of the guards would go on for what seemed like forever, echoing off the mountains. The fiends felt great pleasure in leading the elder to destruction because it was well known among them and Lucre they had no power to destroy the King's children. They could lead the unlearned to destruction but they were powerless to destroy the King's children with their own hands.

For this reason they especially hated Christian. Lucre realized the mistake in bringing the boy into the valley of darkness. Lucre always assigned twice as many fiends to guard Christian. They were to note any who befriended him. "Somehow he must get rid of that boy! To think he had brought the boy into his own dwelling thinking that he could seize the boy's knowledge for his own use."

"Well no matter, he would make an example of his little friend Gayla and then all would either hate him or be too afraid to go near him." Feeling very haughty Lucre congratulated himself for spying out that little traitor who ratted out those stupid enlighten meetings Christian put so much effort in. The only thing made clear by those meetings was the fact that anyone could be bought out. He knew it all along and he would prove it to the King, these precious children were all selfish and self serving. Lucre would prove the children were no nobler than the hogs he kept. At least the hogs didn't try to hide their greed."

"Even the hogs wouldn't take that hot burning liquid the elders loved. The elders took it because of a selfish need to feel good. The silly children would do anything to feel good. Let them drink the poison it provided pleasure for his guards."

Lucre knew why the children were always searching for a good feeling. He was well aware of the separation between the King and the children and he knew why there was no rest for them. Only by connecting to the King would the children find rest. Until that happen, they would always feel something was missing and he did not intend that to happen.

Drinking to search for the peace they long for the elder worker would become reflective of a time long ago. A time only remembered by the spirit. Permitted into the yard, being full of despair and sadness, he would tell the tale of old to all who would listen. Although drunk, the elders were mindful to avoid the guards and never let them hear the tale of how Lucre had once lived in a beautiful Kingdom of peace. But Lucre being full of greed and jealousy turned traitor because he wanted his own beautiful Kingdom. He wanted to be King. After he was expelled, Lucre convinced many of the King's helpers to come away with him after promising, "If you will follow me, I will give you your desires." Lucre said, "I know a way to create and I can get the children to help obtain your desires. The children will agree because they will not be required to obey all the rules the King requires." Then Lucre told the children, "I will show you how to use your power to get all things for yourselves."

The elder went on to explain, "Lucre brought the naïve children and his foolish cohorts to this valley and immediately began trying to imitate the King. Lucre formed and shaped many of the beautiful birds that were found in the King's garden. Lucre took much care to shape each one and to try and match the beautiful colors." As the elder told his tale, he spoke of birds in the King's Kingdom that could sing and soar high into the air. The elder told of "birds that landed on the shoulders of the children and walked around with them all day."

All these things seemed impossible to the younger children. Why they had never seen or heard a bird. It was difficult to imagine anything of beauty in this place. There were no birds here. Then the elder explained, "Lucre's creations were form only. Lucre thought he was so smart in running away to create his own Kingdom. He found some measure of success in stealing the children's minds but he could not use their power to create and he had not the power to give life. He was stuck with his lifeless forms."

The elder loved to imitate how Lucre had scream when he discovered the creative powers of the children required authority from the King to produce. "Lucre stood in the ash covered path wailing his bony little arms in the air shouting, "I will be King!" Sure he could imitate forms and shapes, but Lucre could not give or create life. All life originates with the King and there is set principles to reproduce life. To reproduce life in addition to form or body, you need to be able to give spirit. The spirit we once had. All things exist in the Kingdom of the King by His spirit, the same spirit given to the first man by the King. Lucre had no part of the King's spirit and could not withdraw of it."

Then the elder began to cry and said, "We are forever parted from the King because we choose to follow Lucre. There is nothing left but to join the others in the sleep that never ends." Having said this, the elder looked forlorn and empty.

Now the spirit the elder spoke of was pure and undefiled awaiting authority form the King's word. That's because spirit was before all things created. The King being the original spirit, and the spirit of man came from the King. Man's spirit was empowered with authority from the King by way of the King's word. The King's word and spirit has power over all things, seen and unseen, including the form used to encase the spirit.

When authority was released the spirit would enter into the form designated thus giving it life. The form was energized by man's soul which was called blood. But it is the King's spirit which gives life. Without the King's spirit, the blood remains lifeless. The King's word directed the King's Spirit to give life to man long ago, but Lucre did not have permission to use the King's word and he could not direct the King's spirit which is required for life. He could not direct into the bodily form and he could not direct it out the bodily form. Only the King can do that.

Lucre could only make copies of forms. No matter how beautiful the form, without a spirit, it remains lifeless. But Lucre didn't find this out until much later after he had made a fool of himself in front of all creation. When Lucre discovered he could not use the power given to the King's beloved children to create life he hated the King's children.

Lucre spent many days trying to bring life to this Village only to be surrounded by decay and dead things. It was only later Lucre realized you can only create in your image, each to his own kind; Lucre's time was limited, he was decaying and dying, so that was all he could create. After his humiliation, knowing his time was short, Lucre's one goal became to convince the King's children that they too were in a state of decay and dying.

The King had proven to Lucre that there was only one King and He would always provide for His children. This made Lucre miserable and he wanted to steal the joy of the children too. But first he would have to separate the children from the King.

Lucre began making daily trips back over to the King's Kingdom to entice the children to follow him. He lied about his beautiful Kingdom where there were no rules and everyone could do as they pleased. Many of the children in a moment of curiosity believed Lucre enough to follow him. The journey along the way was always so beautiful. Lucre made sure there was entertainment and pleasure for each one.

It wasn't until they entered the village and found it was covered by blacken ash which fell constantly they knew they had been tricked. But by that time no one knew how to get back to the King and his Kingdom. They felt trapped and full of despair.

The ones who had not fallen asleep became sad hopeless elders. If the elder reciting the tale was caught, he could be beaten and tortured until he gives up his spirit to fall asleep, hoping for peace from the torture. The elder would never wake up. This was the only knowledge the children had of why they came to be here. Many had never seen the King's Kingdom and for those who had seen the Kingdom, they could no longer remember how to get back.

Now Christian had been entrusted with the great task of presenting the truth to the children and at times even he struggled to remember. This place was designed to wipe all thought of the King and his Kingdom from the mind of the children. But the King had planted His truth deep within the heart of each child. So long as each child did not harden his heart, the truth would stay in the warm, loving environment of the heart and survive. There it would blossom giving joy to the owner, waiting to be called into the world.

Only the truth of the King's provision would free the children and ultimately save their very life. The provision that give them total freedom from all bondage and brought them back to the originally state of Royalty they were created in. Christian had to make sure first that the children knew they were free and second that they believed. Truth was the treasure they had hidden deep within their heart. Once they believed they could call it forth by speaking, but each would have to speak it for themselves. Only then could they take their rightful place of superiority over all creation.

Rising from the Altar where he came to talk to the King, Christian no longer felt unsure of himself or the outcome of today's challenge. While emptying the tears from his eyes, he had also emptied all fear and doubt from his heart. Yes there had been doubt hidden under his bravery. Only by running to the King had the doubt had been exposed. When exposed to the truth, fear diminished and doubt was exchanged for the courage of the King. He was glad that instead of running from the problem, he had run to the King.

The unseen presence of the King had forced reality into the spirit of Christian. Although unseen the King's powerful had presence had been felt. A calm peace had invaded not only the cave but also Christian's heart and mind. It felt as if he had been bath in cleansing water.

All negative forces had been dispelled. Light had replaced darkness in the recesses of the boy's mind. He was becoming a force to respect. Just as the King was to be revered, his child was to be respected.

Christian stood up full of power and renewed in the knowledge that the evil holding his brothers and sisters captive in this place would be conquered. It did not appear so, but he had seen and tasted victory deep within. Because he was a son of the King, he was a dominator. It was only a matter of time before all would see.

Leaving the cave and his makeshift Altar, Christian walked back to the hog trough. He did not run.

CHAPTER THREE

Who is the King?

Christian had been such a little boy when Lucre had stolen him away from the King's Kingdom. Now twelve, he stood on the threshold of manhood and sometimes it felt like such a heavy weight on his shoulders; he thought it impossible to carry on. But always the moment passed and he eagerly sought to tell the others of his Father while waiting for him to come and rescue them. You see even before Gayla was taken, Christian was always certain that any day his Father would come for them. Christian was sure, because he knew his Father loved him. To understand the depth of such a love I must try to make you understand a little of Christian's father, the King.

Christian remembered his Father promising to be with him always. "I will never leave, nor forsake you, my son," his Father said. Christian knew his Father never lied so he did not doubt that his Father was near. There was also the time he had commanded Christian to be "strong and of good courage; be not afraid, neither be dismayed; for I the King will be with you wherever you go." It was at that time that Christian had learned he inhibited two worlds through his father. One a world created for him and the other children to rule over and the other where only the King would rule forever. But it was through that world that the King was always near. That world was the spirit realm.

Now my young reader, I will tell you of Christian's Father. Too understand the spirit realm you will need to know who the King is. I have told you a little of Lucre, but there is very little of Lucre to tell. Lucre had his end already in sight. However the King is the beginning and the end of all. Shall we go to the beginning?

Our story begins way back in the beginning of time. At a time and place where everything was dark and gloomy, consisting of one big glop. In the black glop was chaos. There was neither shape nor form in the midst of the empty black space. The blackness spread on for as far as one could see. (If there had been anyone there to see.) But there was no one there to see, except one. The King was there, for this reason the King is known as the Ancient of Days. The King was there before the darkness, because he was first. The King existed with himself and by himself long before anything else came into being. His life force consisted of Royal thoughts, his Royal voice and the Royal spirit. Together the three were one. They each needed the other, but the voice and the spirit reacted to the thoughts, to give them power and direction. The voice gave life to the spirit when the King spoke. In other words the power of the spirit moved when the Royal voice spoke His thoughts. This released power because the Royal voice was the authority the spirit needed to move. If the King did not use his voice, no power could be released and the spirit would remain still. Thoughts provided plans but it was the voice that took the plans to next stage of creating substance.

When the King was ready to create, he had to make a decision to speak His thoughts. Thoughts by themselves did not move the spirit, but once they became Royal words, they were firmly established by the spirit. Now be reminded there is a big difference between thinking and silent speech.

Thoughts and thinking are forms of belief, whereas speech whether verbal or silent is a form of communication. It takes Royal speech to give life to belief through the power of the Royal spirit and one must be of the King's blood line to speak Royal speech. In this same way the King would later create children who operate under the same principle. The children had to know the difference between thought and speaking but most of all they needed to recognize they were of Royal blood.

Order was needed to dispel the chaos so the King set a system of order in place. To achieve order the King established laws and principles for organization. By establishing principles to be applied to all creation, the King decreed how His creation would function. Each decree became the Royal law. The King already knew the purpose He had for everything that he would create.

The King knew the purpose although he had not made his creation because He saw how he intended each individual creation to perform. He had a purpose for every creation. You see the King sees the end result before he makes the beginning.

That is the way the King created His children to live also. He had a purpose for his children. They were to be like him in every way. The King's children were always to envision the end desire they wanted through the thought process, then the desired thing could be established by speaking the outcome or end desire.

With that in mind listen how the King created a world out of chaos. When the King spoke, power from His word made his spirit move. His spirit created everything the King spoke.

Now the King gave his children a voice, but he also gave them a spirit? Not just any spirit but His Royal spirit. Neither the King's spirit nor the children's spirit was visible in this world. The King's spirit was not made of things from this world and the children's spirit was part of His spirit. The King's Spirit was love and so love was planted inside the children.

However the King created forms from the substance of the world. In this way the children were a part of the world they were to rule. Their spirit would live inside the form and always be in contact with the King but the form would do the work to maintain the created world. The King gives the form a name, he called it a body and within this body the spirit and the soul came together. The soul was the third part of the King's children and allowed for them to think by supplying Royal blood the children's mind.

Remember the King was made of thought, spirit and voice. Now His children were thought, spirit and voice, the same as He. Because they were able to think they were able to believe. Just like the King, whatever they believed, the spirit would create so it was very important they believed only good things.

Now the King being love, all His thoughts are good; therefore the children were created to think on whatever was pure and uplifting to the spirit, the spirit being that part of the King which lived inside the children. There could be no evil in the children, only good if the King's Spirit was to stay inside the children because this was the connecting point between them.

The children were meant to be part of two worlds. They were to have their own world, the earth to rule while remaining one with the King in the spirit world. The children would dominate their world through the authority of the King when they spoke His word. In this way the King was also in charge in the children's world because only his word had authority to cause change.

The King ordered His children to love right from the beginning. This was because just like the King, the children released authority to unseen spirits when they spoke words. So long as they obeyed everything would function just as the King purposed. However speaking negative words would give power to negative spirits. Living in a physical world would not take away from their ruler ship in the spirit world. This was an advantage to being the King's child.

Now the King is only one spirit and can not join with other spirits. The King's spirit must remain pure and unadulterated. His very essence is love. Love is the only true spirit because the King is creator of all things. For this reason, love always looks out for others. Love is the substance of the King and every thing he does is out of love. To have fellowship with the King the children had to reject every spirit that was not born of love. Not only did they have to reject the renegade spirits, there would also come a time when the children would have to war against the renegade spirits.

It was the spirit of love that motivated the King to want someone to love. So what does he do? He says, "let us make man in our image." Now the King meant he wanted children just like him. That meant they would abide by the sprit of love, like the King. They would have power in their words because he would give them a part of His spirit to follow the idea behind their words. Everything the King had, he gave to his children because he wanted them to be like him.

The King spoke everything into existence; but for His children he would create them in His image. Every spoken word of the King must do exactly what He says. If the children were spoken into existence, they would not be able to choose for themselves and they would not be rulers like the King. The King is great because He chooses to love. The Children must be able to choose because someday they might be presented with a choice that would require them to know how great they were because of their Father's greatness.

The King was pleased; he would have children he could give all his love to. The King wanted to make a place for his children before they came. All parents want a special place for their young and the King was no different. Parents run all around and pick out paint for the room, buying curtains and pretty furniture to get everything ready before the baby comes. That's what the King did. He picked colors, flowers, and everything for his children. But he did not call his creation a nursery, because it was to be much bigger, The King created a domain for his children and they were to be in dominion over the entire domain.

Such joy had never been felt on the earth before. The King poured his love into his words and beautiful words came through his voice. As he spoke the joy He felt was infused into all the things spoken into existence. Joy was the cement which the foundation of creation was held together with. The foundation was love. There was no room for sadness in this domain.

The King spoke of gleaming, sparkling waterfalls with clear blue streams. He spoke of bright blue skies with fluffy white clouds. The King spoke of lights in the sky for day, which he called the Sun and lights in the sky for night called the stars and the moon. Everything the King spoke appeared just as he said. Nothing can deny the King, when He speaks, it must be just as he said. That's why the King said few words. When the King speaks, it is just as He says; there is no argument with the King's word. All creation agrees with the King.

The sound of the King's voice was like beautiful music radiating throughout the land as he spoke. The King's voice was the first melody ever heard and someday His children would use music to reverence Him. The King chooses His words carefully for their intended purpose. The children were to use their words in the same way. Never were words to be used in frivolous manner, they were too powerful.

When the King said let there be light, then just like that, there was light! The Sun appeared without hesitation. Because the King spent so much time alone with his word and his spirit, the King didn't have to talk all the time. You see they were all in agreement from the moment of thought. The King wanted just such closeness with his children. His children were to be of one mind with him.

Now when the King had spoken for light and the Sun and the Moon appeared and the King in his wisdom divided each to one half of the sky. The King likes order and organization, that's why he put a season and a time to everything under the Sun. The King placed the stars with the moon because the Moon was not as bright as the Sun. He called the side with the Sun, the day and the side with the Moon and stars, he called night. After everything was hung in its proper place, the King called the entire thing, heaven. Then He declared laws to regulate the function of the heavens.

After he had completed the heavens, he divided sparkling waters and placed dry land in different sections of the water. God commanded the earth to bring forth vegetation and for every plant to produce seed of it's own kind. The King decreed everything would reproduce of its own kind in the form of seed. The seen and the unseen, the mental and the physical would all reproduce. This included the thoughts of man.

He commanded seed for every thing according to the established law; nothing could stop seed time and harvest time so long as the worlds exist. This was a decree of the King. However if a physical form no longer supplied a need, the King could cause all production of the form to cease and it would die out. That's because nothing in the physical world was permanent, only the spiritual world was permanent, including the spirit of mankind. The King intended His children to live forever.

However when mankind later lost dominion, the King cease production of some of the larger animals. The safety and continuation of mankind for the intended purpose of the King was precedence and just as all things were in subjection to the children; all things could be sacrificed for the children also. The only thing not in subjection to the children of the King was the other children. All the children were equal because all were created in the image of the King and all were equally loved.

What a beautiful domain the King had made. Bright Sunshine upon sparkling waters and dry lands too. Twinkling stars and soft moonlight were on the other side. The King looked and said, "It is good." . The creation of the King is the beginning of the unchangeable truth and because the King is just it is also the end. What he has decreed shall remain forever, world without end.

Once it is understood that truth originated with the King, we can appreciate that He cannot lie. Then it is evident "that things which are seen were made of things which do not appear." Hammers, nails or any tools were used to form this domain, only the Word of the King. This may be hard to imagine, until we understand that truth originates and ends with the King. Remember he was first, so he determines what is real.

Now that the King had flowers, trees, grass and beautiful fruits, there beautiful colors everywhere. These were truth.

Next the King spoke to the waters to bring forth moving creatures and of course the waters had to obey. There were fish swimming and jumping in the sunlight, splashing clear water droplets in the air. The King also commanded for birds that could fill the air to come forth. There were large birds with baldheads, but of course they weren't really bald, they only look bald because the feathers on their head were white. There were small blue birds that sang pretty songs and over near the waterfall, there were brown birds with red breast. There were so many and they were all full of joy!

Then he created great sea monsters and other living creatures that moved. All these the waters brought forth. These too were truth.

The King looked about at the fish, the fowl, and the vegetation; he spoke to them saying, "Be fruitful and multiply." The King looked with approval and said, "It was good."

Next the King spoke to the dry land. The King told the dry land to produce the beast, cattle and all manner of creeping things. Proof! Up sprang animals and insects in less than a second. What the King spoke came to be because this was the beginning of truth.

Horses, bugs, great big creatures with large bodies and small heads; creatures with horns and long ivory tusks appeared in an instant. Some had hoofs, some had claws and some hopped on two legs. There were creatures with fur, creatures with rough skin; brown creatures, striped animals, spotted animals, all variety of animals.

The King looked at all that he spoke into being and "it was good." The love of the King could be felt everywhere. You could hear the King's love in the songs the birds sang and you could feel the King's love in the soft gentle breeze as it lightly moved through the tall grass. You could smell the King's love in the flowers.

The King's love was everywhere, from the warm glow of the Sun to the cool touch of the clear blue waters. This was a happy place. The King instructed the animals to go and produce their own kind. Furry animals would produce furry animals and striped animals would produce striped animals. Animals with horns would produce babies that would grow horns. Some would be different colors, but each would resemble the first. The first has the most power and everything that follows the first is in the image of the first.

The King had changed what was dark and gloomy into a beautiful domain for his children. IT WAS TIME TO CREATE HIS CHILDREN.

When the King had created the dry land, he put into the dirt all the component parts needed to make things grow and live, except for water, which he had made first. But the King had set the dry land upon the water so that the there was moisture in the dirt. Everything created by the King either supported life or produced life.

The earth had the ingredients; the Sun produced the light to give energy to the earth's ingredients and water to supply oxygen and nourishments for growth. The King knew every thing his children would need and all things were made to achieve the needs of his children. He created all things with his children in mind, because He loved them even before he made them. The King was looking at what would be the end result of all creation.

During the times when the King lived alone with his voice and his spirit, it was not necessary to speak because the three of them knew what the other ones wanted. But all the while the King was creating the domain for his children; he spoke everything he wanted. In this way creation and the laws which govern it were established. "In the presence of two or three a thing shall be decreed and so it shall be established." The King, his voice and his spirit were three in one, so all his creation was established in the presence of these three. The King's children were meant to be rulers over all the domain of earth by order of the King. This was the home the King created for his children.

Now let us proceed. The King, his voice and his spirit were three in one, so all his creation was established in the presence of these three. Now that it was time to make the children of the King and what does the King do? He speaks! The King said "Let us make man in our image." Power came forth when the King spoke.

Now the King speaks "Let us make man in our image," and the power goes forth, but notice what the King said. He didn't say bring forth man, he said let us make man. This was different, the King wanted to make his child. The King takes the earth he created and begins to mold and shape a form for the man-child. The King lovingly shapes the body with love. With a gentle caress here, a loving touch to form his lips, and in tenderness he smoothes the eyebrows of His beloved until the man child was fashioned.

The King holds the man-child gentle because he is so precious. And when the King had formed and shaped the man-child completely, the King leaned into the face of the man-child and as he leaned in; He softly covered the nose and mouth of the man-child with his very essence and breathe life into the man-child.

We spoke of water giving oxygen and nourishment to the dirt to grow and sustain life. Here we see the King fashion a man-child from the dirt and instead of pouring water upon him to make grow; the King breathes the living water of his spirit into him and the man-child comes to life. Because the King is life.

The King was pleased. The King looked at his son and spoke, "See all things were created for you. Go and name the animals, trees and flowers. Call them what you wish." The King felt such love for this child; he had someone to give him joy and pleasure.

After many days the King created a she-child. The King knew the joy of having someone to love and he wanted his man-child to know that same joy. So He created a she-child for the man-child to love and to fulfill her function. This time the man-child did not name the creation, the King named her himself. He called her woman.

The King commanded the man and woman to multiply and produce more children. The King wanted a big family to love. The King said, "It is good." How the King loved his children. He wanted them to be happy in this earthly place. The domain he created for them to dominate and rule.

And so it was for many years. Until Lucre wanted to be King.

In the beginning the children were very aware of their spirit and just like the King; they used the King's words to rule in love over the new world. Christian knew this because he had been taught all these things, but Lucre knew because he desired these things for himself.

Lucre also knew that the children's spirit would follow the command of their words and thoughts. For this reason Lucre surmised he needed to cause confusion in the minds of the children in order to gain control of the children. Since everything created by the King operated on truth, Lucre spoke lies.

Just as Lucre was not part of the King, the lie was not part of truth. Whereas truth generates life and freedom, the lie caused death and bondage. The lie could not create death and bondage, but it could lead to it. The lie was the only thing Lucre originated. The lie was originated to steal the right to rule.

Because the King created all things out of truth, truth is necessary for a thing to operate in its intended purpose. Truth is the principle necessary for the child of the King to operate in authority. Without truth Lucre could destroy their right to rule by blocking their authority. Then he could become ruler over them and compel them to use their power for his use.

To accomplish this he would first make them think on untrue things, thus directing believeth in that direction. Once they believed the untrue thing, they would be compelled to give power to the lie by speaking believeth in the lie. The children applied Royal words to an untruth causing their words to be an abomination to the King. The authority given by the King was void.

Once he had convinced the children to believe the lie it could exist until it was exposed to truth. All truth was encompassed in the King's words so without the King's words the children would never be able to expose the lie to the truth of the King's word.

So Lucre began a plan to separate the children from the King and to strip their authority to rule. Separation would prevent them from knowing the King's word. Without knowledge of the King's words, the children would have no knowledge of truth and the lies could cause them to destroy themselves by malfunction.

When the King established order, even He was subjected to the regulations he put in place. The one way to cause separation between the King and his children was to persuade the children to violate or disobey the decrees of the King. To disobey the King would constitute anarchy and rebellion against the King. This would unite the children with evil. Lucre knew no matter how much the King loved them; the King could have no part of wickedness and would have to inflict punishment on the children which fit the crime. Punishment could include separation and eventually death. There can be no life without the King. But Lucre did not know how deep the King's love was.

So he set out to plant negative thoughts in the minds of the children, causing them to speak the negative thoughts. Then he would accuse them of wrong all day and all night until they were destroyed through self condemnation for not being what the King created them to be. At that point they would embrace wickedness and reject their Royal status, never knowing that by doing so they were embracing Lucre and rejecting the King. They would choose Lucre's lies over the King's truth of who they were. In this way he, Lucre would be their true ruler. All these things Lucre planned because he desire to be King.

He would cause insurgency by giving rise to jealousy, anger and hatred. These too were spirits. They were radical spirits, followers of Lucre, revolting against God. These spirits like all spirits, could achieve power only after being activated by the children's words. Words were seeds and because of the principle the King set over them, they would reproduce after their own kind.

Therefore words spoken in jealousy, anger and hatred would continue to produce long after they were spoken. The only way to stop their reproduction was to kill them with truth. Radical words had to be counteracted with the truth of the situation or the person as spoken by the King. The King's truth produce righteousness and therefore it produced good. The King's spoke righteousness over all creation right from the very beginning. Righteousness resulting when truth is put in effect by speaking will neutralize spoken evil.

The decree of seed time and harvest time declared by the King stated that whatever was planted would yield a harvest of its own kind. Lucre's plan was for the children to plant evil sinful spirits with their words. Spirits that were under his command and eventfully would overtake the King's spirit of love if his plan worked out as he planned.

CHAPTER FOUR

Lucres Folly

The King was very proud of his children. The days and evening were spent in companionship and joy. The King watched the man-children take charge of their world, making decisions and plans for the earth and its inhabitants. Not only for the earth but the children made decisions to help each other. The children showed love in everything they did.

It was coming up on High Time. High Time was a time of festivals and games. During this time the children showed creative thinking in exercising authority over the earth and in showing love to the other children. It was a time for the children to be receptive to the teachings of the law declared by the King. The children would display their gift to be of one mind with the King.

The children could seek help from their helper. Each child had a guardian spirit to help them at all times. The most popular helper was Lucre. Lucre had a pleasing voice and he above all others was chosen to sing for the King. Everyone loved Lucre, but Lucre was not content with his position in the Kingdom. Lucre had a secret. He wanted to be King.

The festival originated in the lush deep green meadow outside the great forest. Just on the other side of the meadow was the garden called Eden. Although the children were in command over all the earth, their home was the clam serene place of Eden. Eden was a soothing cool place. The temperature was always just right and there was a peaceful ambiance present. Love could be felt all over. There were beautiful waterfalls and birds sang soothing melodies day and night. They sang songs of merriment during the day and cooed calm lullabies during the night. Tall trees for cool shade allowed sunlight to stream into the garden upon the happy family of the King. The children were gifted in many talents. In fact they could sing as beautiful as any bird. It gave the King great pleasure to hear the children praise him with song.

Cyrill was a cheerful, fun loving young man. He loved the King more than anything. Next to love for the King, he loved his friend Aldolphina. Leading came naturally to Cyrill and was his greatest talent. Cyrill was a good leader because of the natural love he felt for all creation. Cyrill loved helping any way he could.

There was only one thing Cyrill needed or desired. It was very important to the young man for Aldolphina to respect him. He needed to be important to her. Oh, he knew she loved him, but he needed her admire him. Cyrill had no idea why her respect was so important; he just knew he needed to please her.

The High Time was especially fun for Cyrill. It was a time to not only help and show care for this world he loved, but it was also a time for special attention from the King. Humming a happy song, Cyrill put the final touch to his project.

"What are you doing," Lucre ask Cyrill? "Look at my plan! I've found a way to protect the eagle's eggs. I love all the birds, but the eagle is so smart. The eagle is the only bird that soars with the wind. It only makes sense that the nest should be placed high up. They're majestic and I want to take care of them. With the eagle's keen eye sight, the nest will be visible from miles away and the little one's climb out to soon. I'll use it as my final presentation.

"Cyrill you're as sharp as the eagle's eyes are keen. I'll bet Aldolphina thinks you're really special?" Lucre had watched the boy when he thought no one was looking. For this reason he knew Cyrill had special feelings for the girl. Stopping suddenly and peering at the ground, Cyrill was almost speaking to himself, "I don't really think she sees me most of the time."

"Jackpot," Lucre thought to himself, but aloud he pressed Cyrill to explain. "The King says we are to put others before ourselves. I'm glad to have His instructions; otherwise I would be very unhappy. I want to be special to Aldolphina but knowing what the King says helps me to be content near her. But I do hope someday she decides she needs my help. Besides love is never pushy."

"Cyrill you are growing more like the King everyday. I'm glad to see you're staying true to the King's Word. Gotta go. I'll see you later."

Lucre was so excited he could hardly contain his laughter. He had been waiting many years for a sign that perhaps there was even a little discontentment among the children. All he needed was for one child to desire something they were unsure of. "If they are unsure then there is doubt. Cyrill has no idea his desire is leading to doubt about a situation. Some ruler he will make. The heart of these children will my passage way into their thoughts. Doubt is the seed I will plant there. It will reach into the mind of the children to alter their thinking," Lucre planned. He continued, "If I can alter the thinking of the children, I can also alter the passage way into the spirit realm. Instead of the lighted path, doubt will open the passage onto the path of darkness and it will yield a harvest for my purpose. The King never intended his precious children to enter into the spirit realm of darkness but with a little encouragement they soon will. Yes it's time I began to acquire my kingdom. I've waited a long time. This will be sweet! I must find Aldolphina and strike quickly."

Aldoplhina was busy working on a project for High Time when Lucre peered around the tree she was under. He strutted over very casual and off-handily he innocently inquired, "What are you doing?" Lucre had developed the skill of putting the children at ease by starting conversation with a question. It made the other party feel in control. One thing about these little Kings, they all loved having the answers. Lucre knew there was no way they had answers for him because they didn't know the real question. The real question was, "Can you be deceived?"

Aldophina barely raised her head as she replied, "I want this to be my best idea ever. I really want to be a help and to please the King." I have to finish. It's almost time to prepare the horses for the Seek and Rescue relay. I've been speaking with Aqualine and it's agreed that we will be partners."

"There should be no need for agreement. Aqualine is a horse and you are the dominator, she must do whatever you command her," Lucre said. "I know I am the dominator, but just as the King gives each of us a choice,

I want her to have a choice in her partner. Surely you know how much I love speaking with all the animals?"

"Besides the race is very important to me and the ending of a win is much greater where there is agreement. The King has spoken many times of the importance of agreement when two or more are involved. Even though I am in charge, even the earth and the animals can be in agreement." Adolphina was looking straight into Lucre's eyes as she spoke the last sentence. She thought she detected something odd in her favorite helper but it was only for a second and she dismissed the thought.

But Lucre was aware the girl had seen him through her spirit eyes and knew that he must avoid getting to close if his plan was to have a chance of success. "The truth is always revealed in the spirit; better keep her attention on the concerns of this world for the moment. Better to finish this up and make a hasty retreat leaving her to think," he was thinking.

The second part of High Time consisted of the Search and Rescue relay which was a Sabbath day's journey circling through the forest, ending on the opposite of the meadow, which was Eden. For this part of the festival the children would be required to journey away from Eden but only for a short time. The trail started at the western edge of the meadow, and would end on the eastern edge after winding through the forest encountering dangerous obstacles. By finishing on the eastern edge, which was the garden, the children would have completed a full circle.

The race was designed to test the children's earthly senses such as sight, hearing, and touch while teaching them to incorporate their spirit essence into every aspect of life. Even though the children were created to inhabit the earth world, they must never lose their spirit ability and they were not to rely on their earthly senses. Their spirit was not only their connection to the King but it was who they were.

Along the way the children would have to exercise their dominion over their environment including any beast they might encounter in order to complete the task. Because the journey was intended to strengthen the children's ability to rule, their competence in the task of ruling would determine the winner. The two key elements the King was looking for were; love and obedience. He hoped for many winners.

Aldolphina was determined to win. She knew it would be necessary to obey all the principles established by the King. Mentally she made a conscience decision to be lead by her spirit and to force her earth being to obey her spirit. The only problem was that the earth being wanted control over what belonged to it, namely the earth. However that was part of the trial, affirming to all creation that the spirit ruled both earth and spirit. Aldolphina looked forward to the fun but still she took her responsibility very serious.

Just as being King carried a great deal of accountability, being a child of the King carried the same accountability. It was important to be a good provider for all those subjected to you. Only then could one be a good ruler.

Lucre began a test of his own on the girl and as always he started with a question. "Aldoplhina you seem to be well ahead of the other children including Cyrill, don't you think you should help him?" Now Lucre knew there that each child had to work on their own, asking help only from their assigned helpers, but he wanted to plant a thought for Cyrill into Aldolphina's mind. He needed her thoughts to be strong in favor of Cyrill.

"Lucre don't you know we can't share strategies before the competition? When the winners are decided then everyone will share the things learned during the event. We abide in all things by the King's rules. Besides I know how inclusive Cyrill is and I have confidence he'll do very well. He'll probably come very close to winning. Why do you ask such a question so obviously against the rules?"

"No, you misunderstood me Aldolphina. I would never suggest you do anything against the King's rules. But I am wiser than you and I only sought to help you as well as Cyrill. The highest principle the King has established is to love one another as you love yourself. It would not be cheating to help Cyrill out of love. Besides just before I came here I was talking to him and he confessed how his feelings are for you. Both his earth being and his spirit essence care deeply for you. I just thought you would like to know. Now I must be on my way, but we'll talk later."

Lucre felt sure the seed of doubt was taking firm root. That was his goal, to plant the seed and watch it grow. "Cyrill is beginning to doubt whether the King's way of contentment will get Aldolphina to respect him and I've planted a seed to cause Aldolphina to ponder whether love will allow her to disobey the King. Now all I need do is travel along the competition watching the two until a circumstance presents itself to test these two in the area of their doubts. Opportunity must be pounced upon," he laughed aloud. "Perhaps neither question was big, but it only required a small seed to produce a big crop. Small seeds of doubt will produce big profits in this scheme to break the bond between the King and His children. I am a master and I will devise a masterpiece out of the right situation for my pleasure. Once I break that bond between the King and the children, they will need me to conduct all their affairs."

The time for the festival arrived and all the children were excited. The first part of the festival happened on the morning of the first day. It was a time of worship to the King. The morning was filled with acts of homage to the King. Included were songs of praise to show appreciation to the King for His love. The children were thankful to the King for the gift of love. Although they had never known anything but love, the spirit inside the children told them love was special. There was no knowledge of what their life would be like without love, but they knew there was a peace and joy over their family that was unexplainable. So for this they were grateful and in turn they freely gave love back to the King.

The music group had practice for weeks on songs filled with words of love for the King. Words were used to paint pretty pictures in the thoughts of all present. As the thoughts were formed they created more love. The songs paid tribute to His greatness.

There was another group selected to dance. The dancers made head bands of every beautiful flower in Eden. There were skirts and tops made entirely of colorful flowers. Color splashed in dazzling display with every dance. The Sun shone brightly and the sky was a special blue. Young children were given rides on fluffy white clouds. Animals of all ages languished in the grass playing with the children. Today the spirit and the earth realm joined together to give honor to the King. On this day everything in creation bowed to the King.

Lucre stood over to the side watching the events unfold. He had a plan for Aldolphina; he was sure her love would be used to his advantage. "The girl was full of love, but did he detect a small amount of pride there also? Was her confidence because she was a child of the King or was her confidence in herself? Well we'll just find out," he thought. Now he would wait for the right moment.

The King looked over all the grounds taking pleasure in the love and care the children had shown in preparing every aspect of the festival. Because he was King, as always he saw the end result of the festival before the beginning. What he saw cause great sadness in him. It would be many years before there would be this kind of joy with the children again. Once this journey began his children would change forever. But he could not prohibit the children from making choices.

However the King gave no place to sadness because he was already speaking the corrective action for the errors he saw coming. Being in control and having power over all things, the King never indulged in thought concerning problems; instead he used his thoughts to guide his words into spoken declarations of what he wished to occur. The children were to use their thoughts in the same way. After all they were made to be like him.

They were never to use time on problems, only corrections. Just as everything was created for the children, time was also at the command of the children. In order for them to learn this, they would have to be presented with choices along the journey. Choices that would be intended to make use of their divine abilities to rule.

These were the King's children, created to rule all things; they would be presented with tough choices. Some of these choices might even lead to their destruction, but there would always be a way of escape from trouble. They had all sufficiency to solve whatever problem they might encounter because He was their father. They only needed to obey the King's instructions by trusting His word. To trust His word they had know His word. The King provided for this by putting His decrees into writing and instructing the children to speak of His words. Success was guaranteed so long as the children followed the King's plan and the journey would end in victory.

Aldolphina would have to decide for herself when the time came, but he would be here to help. However there would be consequences for Lucre's actions when that time came also.

The morning festivities drew to a close and the contestants prepared for the journey. Each child stood beside their mounts and awaited final instructions from their King. Excitement was high and each child wanted to do their best. To find favor with the King give such joy.

Knowing what only he knew, the King prepared to give life saving instructions to his children. Although unseen the King could be heard. The King's loud voice thundered from the sky as He addressed the children. "During your seven day journey you are to put into effect actions to exercise your spirit and your earthly persona to perform appropriate to your created s. You are rulers over all creation. You are made only a little lower than me. It is expected that you will represent me in all your actions, thoughts and behavior. You must follow my instructions and never turn from my orders if you are to succeed. I have made provisions for every need you will encounter on your journey. You have the right to use the provisions, but you can only access the provisions when you apply the established principles to your actions to achieve your desired results."

"The main principle at work in this earth is seeding and harvesting. You live in a garden because a garden is where seeds are planted. You must make this entire earth your garden. Seeding is applied to all your thoughts and speech. You are the carrier of all seed."

"You possess the ability to choose different components to induce your seed to grow. The one component is faith, is a natural part of who are and will give you the desired result of victory. Faith is a natural part because it is an ingredient of the part of myself I put in you. You are to speak only that which is allowed my law for the betterment of yourself and others. That is the purpose of this journey, to serve yourself and others in love. If love is present you will obey my instructions without fault."

"The other factor, doubt is available only through choice. This factor will cause you to disobey and if you continue to disobey, soon you will cease to love me. However we are each a part of the other and when you cease to love me, you cease to love that part of you which is of me. If you stay in such a state long enough you will self destruct. Doubt is not part of your natural makeup and has no part with me. It would have to be chosen to be present."

"This factor will ensure failure for you. You decide which result you want, but beware that your actions are useless if they do not support your choice. Both components require speech to release its growth potential."

"You have been given the set of laws you need for life, but you cannot use them if you are not on familiar terms with them. In that case they will be of no help to you and you will limit my ability to help you. I will not break the law to help you. As King I must be just and operate according to the declared decrees I have set in place. If you follow the rules we will all be justified and you can complete the journey according to my plan. Your steps and actions will be analyzed at different stages through out the journey. If rules have been violated you will be given instructions to make corrections. If discipline is required it will be to help you do better and grow stronger. The journey was not purposed for failure but for growth resulting in perfection. There will be no need for defense because there can be no accusation against any. Obey my instructions,"

"Proceed and keep my decrees. Although you will not see me, I will always be here for you."

With that the children began to ride out, one by one to begin the journey that would characterize their ruler ship over the earthly world given them by their King. The journey had begun.

Although each of the children was destined for the same destination there were many routes within the forest available for them to choice. It was up to each to decide their route; however the rules were the same for all routes. They could also choose to make the journey alone or with a partner. If they choose a partner each partner had to travel the same route and ride together. The two would be scrutinized as one.

Both Cyrill and Aldolphina were making the journey alone.

Cyrill felt excitement upon entering the forest. The way was well lighted Cyrill like the thought of being in charge of his trip. The riders all waved to each other smiling and shouting as they began. There was much laughter and merriment among all the children. Each child started on their journey.

Aldolphina was first to pull ahead of the others. They were still in sparse growth and the horse was able to spread her legs. Wind wrestling in her braids, Aldolphina rode high on her mount. Power and confidence vibrated in every cell of her being. Leaves rustled as she passed and earth was churned and tossed in the air with every step of the horse. Everything in her world was as the creator intended. It was as though all nature bowed before her as she passed. Aldolphina was in charge of her world.

Others spread out in all directions on this predestined journey. There was excitement as well as security at knowing where they were headed but being free to choose how they would get there. It was with confidence they traveled, after all the King would watch over them. How could they go wrong?

Several challenges were presented all along the journey. Some challenges were small and some were large. Each challenge presented the opportunity to make the right choice and advance on.

Stephanie and Jessie were not long on the trail before they encountered trouble. The two had chosen to travel together but disagreement arose about a turn in the rode. The rule for partnership required agreement in all things. It was getting late in the day and they had been stalled at this one place because neither would compromise.

Stephanie wanted to turn west and Jessie felt it wiser to go east. The King had commanded that "The Sun should never settle with their being angry or resentful," yet here they set unable to move forward because of selfness. Many of the other children could be heard passing them by off in the distance.

Finally realizing how far behind they were falling, Stephanie said, "Alright, we'll do it your way. Lead the way!" The two started down the path chosen by Jessie with Jessie feeling he had won a battle. Stephanie felt resentful at having given in. The Sun was just setting and although they were once again moving forward, neither gave thought to the King's law.

Stephanie did not make her decision out of obedience to the King's rule, but because she didn't want to lose. She carried the resentment with her as the Sun set.

Earlier in the day Charlie had come across a boulder in the path chosen by him. Charlie had spent hours devising a pulley system that would move the boulder. Muscles taunt and a body with the precision of the universe, Charlie stayed with the project until he moved the boulder. Never once did he speak his authority over the blockage in his path, but still he caused the boulder to move. He was so proud of his handiwork. What was more important was how proud the King would be of him. "By his own self, he had solved this problem and was ready for the next. HA! Let's see someone top that. Pretty soon he would hardly need to call on the King at all."

With much joy Charlie jumped on the back of his horse and prepared to trot off down his chosen trail, never looking back. Had Charlie looked back, he would seen the man made pulley coming loose and he would have avoided the boulder from hitting his horse on the hind end. Charlie and the horse lay injured on the trail. Still Charlie did not speak his authority over the situation.

The children encountered many obstacles throughout the journey and each child continued on. None would quit. In their hearts they determine they were Royalty in control of their journey and they would finish. During the first part of the journey each day they would approach the King to request His help, but as the journey went on and they grew near their destination it became later in the day before they would go to the King.

However the King always stayed near, watching over the children, ready to help when they ask. The King saw the mistakes the children made, but knowing the power he had given them, he was more interested in the corrections they made. After all their spirit could correct any wrong the earth body caused. That was the importance of the journey; learning to place the spirit above the earth body.

The mistakes did not matter, what mattered is that the mistakes were made because they did not follow his instructions. Once the spirit was placed first, the instructions would come naturally. The decrees were automatic to their spirit, but the earth body did not understand the decrees. If they were to be true princes they would have to follow the Royal decrees. Even the King was bound by the Royal decrees.

Both Cyrill and Aldophina excelled at following the King's orders. They remembered to command the waters and the winds to help during their travels. The squirrels would bring nuts for them to enjoy and the trees bent their arms to offer fruit. Everything created by the King was at their discretion and they knew the principle relevant for the results they desired. The two relied on the King's instructions to progress on their journey and it wasn't long before they were way ahead of the others. That's when they met at the same point on the journey. By that time they were almost totally depending on the spirit, using their earth senses only rarely.

Because both of the children truly loved one another they were happy to see that they were ahead of the others. Oh now don't think they didn't love the others because they did. These two loved everyone and everything. They were pleasing to the King.

It was for this reason that Lucre had targeted them to hurt the King.

Jumping from his horse Cyrill laughed while helping Aldolphina to the ground. Twirling in ecstasy the two embraced. Overhead the Sunlight sprinkled through the leaves of the trees. Beneath their feet the soft grass wrapped around their bare feet giving cool comfort and tickling their toes. The smell of freshly watered grass permeated the children's nose. Moisture oozed form the ground to sooth the earth and replenish all growing things. The shadows within the forest were friendly and inviting for the young people. All was quiet waiting for the command of the man-children. All creation gave evidence of the King's greatness and they were His children.

Perhaps it was the exhilaration and satisfaction of having completed so much of their journey. After all it was now late in the second day and there had been few problems. The King had spoken his approval at the progress along the way and the entire world was truly at their command.

Lucre knew the time to strike had come. He knew the best time to lie was when the truth was sparkling integrity and honesty upon conditions. The glare of the truth would shield the lie. Yes it was true they were in charge because they were children of the King, but it was also because they were children of the King that they must obey the laws of the King.

Speaking to Aldolphina, Cyrill suggested a celebration. "Let's prepare a special feast tonight. Something we've never eaten before. It's one earth sense still prevailing. The desire for good food," he laughed. "The whole forest is at our disposal, we can choose whatever we want." "Yes, let's do that, Aldolphina agreed. "You search that way and I'll go this way. Bring back your choice and I'll give you my choice."

"Oh, you need a new challenge so soon. Aldolphina that's one of the things I love most about you. You find joy in everything. There is always excitement when you're around."

Cyrill darted out of sight behind one of the big trees. He was more than a little embarrassed at having blurted so much of his thought out. The feelings he had for Aldolphina were so strong. There was a change going on in him and he wasn't sure if he liked it. Aldolphina had always been special but now she occupied a lot of his thought. So much that during times he had reserved for the King's Word he would find her presence in his mind. "It wasn't important as soon as High Time was over he would talk to the King," he thought to himself.

Walking along humming to herself, Aldolphina looked carefully at all the choices available to her. "The King is so good. Everywhere I look, I see his love. I am special because of His love." The young girl started to sang out loud overcome by all the wonderful things that came from the King's thoughts. Every taste, every size and color all were the results of His loving thoughts for His family. How she loved him.

Never giving thought to Cyrill, her love was concentrated on the goodness of the King. It wasn't that she didn't love Cyrill; she wasn't aware of the change taking place in Cyrill. There was something new and different going on in Cyrill. Briefly she reflected, "Cyrill is really getting strange. The competition was really straining his thought process."

Lucre had travel along with the children in spirit form through out the trip. The King had given orders to the helpers to be available to help the children at all times. Now Lucre and the other helpers had the ability to metamorphose. To transform required permission from the King, but because of the festival, approval had been given for the helpers to change forms if needed to help the children. But Lucre chose to remain unseen during this part of the journey.

Knowing how much Aldolphina loved the animals, Lucre changed into a serpent. Just as she communicated with her horse very efficiently,

Aldolphina was especially gifted to speak with all the animals. Each of the animals had an important role here in their wonderful home and she loved each species.

Lucre ambled up to Aldolphina in his transformed state and asks, "What are you looking for." Looking as radiant as Sunshine, love gleamed all over her smiling face, "Hello Sir Serpent. I am looking for an especially divine food fit for a Princess," she laughed. The serpent said, "Well you should. The whole forest has heard of the magnificent job you and Cyrill have done. Surely you deserve a meal fit for a King. There is a special food on yonder tree. It's never been sampled by anyone before. You would be special if you were to eat it."

"Looking in the direction indicated by the serpent, Aldolphina gasp in surprise. "Don't you know that tree is forbidden by the Royal edict issued by the King? No one is to eat of that tree, lest they enter into the world of darkness and death. Everyone knows the world of darkness can have no part with the King or His children."

"You have nothing to fear of the darkness. Are you not in charge over all things? The King is King over everything. He knows that you too have dominion over darkness. The King is only waiting for you to excel in spirit living before allowing you to assist him in control of the darkness. You're almost there now. Just think how proud he'll be of you when you complete this journey. It will please him to know you have taken control over darkness also. The King knows that once you eat that fruit, you will be as much in charge as He is. Don't you want to be as great as He? Eat the fruit and show the King how much you are like him."

Aldolphina wanted so much to show the King how she had excelled in all in instructions, now she could surprise him by becoming just like him. Why she could help him if she knew all that he knew. Didn't this food grow from seed like all food? Surely it was from good seed. Quickly Aldolphina snatched the fruit and began to eat it.

Several hours passed before Cyrill returned. But time was of no importance in creation. Creation like the spirit realm was not bound by time. No one ever grew impatient.

Cyrill could be heard whistling as he rounded the corner. His arms were loaded with the good fruit of the forest. "There were so many original fruits he had never tasted and he was anxious to sample them all, except the one fruit forbidden by the King. Of course he would never want to make the King angry. The King is very generous to provide us with so many varieties, He never withholds any good thing from us," Cyrill thought. Thoughts of thankfulness to the King filled his head as he walked.

Upon rounding the corner and coming into plain sight of Aldolphina, the boy's jaw dropped as well as every fruit he carried. "NO!" Screaming for his friend to stop, Cyrill charged at the hand holding the forbidden fruit. But even as the fruit fell to the ground, he could see he was too late. Large bites had been taken and he could see Aldolphina swallowing the remains left in her mouth. "What have done?" his whispered. The disbelief at what had just transpired before his eyes made Cyrill's voice barely audible.

For the first time Aldolphina listen to the misgivings she had ignored in her head. Wanting to justify her actions she looked around to the serpent for support. Strangely he was no where to be seen. Looking back at Cyrill's anguished face, she mustered up a confidence she didn't feel. Although her eyes belied her true doubt, she squared her shoulders in defiance and spoke, "There was nothing wrong with eating of this fruit. It is splendid and we are entitled to all the forest has. Besides the serpent said the King was going to allow us the fruit when we had successfully completed the journey to His satisfaction. You said we would have a special feast so I choose a special fruit."

As Aldolphina spoke, there was a change taking over every feature of her face and body. Cyrill could see the change and Aldolphina felt it in her heart. The girl gave up all pretense of defiance and began to cry with a longing that was strange and new to her. Cyrill had never heard such longing before. He needed to comfort her, but what could he do. Both children knew the grievous error the girl has committed. It was well known that the King's commands were to be followed, but it was not known what effect to willfully disobey would have. They had never dared to disobey the King. Sure there had been learning experiences, but this was outright rebellion and the thought of the consequences was too great for either to think. For the first time they felt fear. Fear was not of the King and it had no place in the children.

"What can we do Ally, Cyrill ask?" The new term for her was his way of conveying how dear she was to him. "Cyrill if you eat some too perhaps the King won't be so mad, Aldolphina said as she held the fruit out to her young friend."

Cyrill looked at the fruit and then into the eyes of this girl so close to his heart. He wanted to help her, to comfort her. Cyrill wanted no doubt regarding his feelings about her. She was so beautiful even in this new and strange state. What had changed her? Looking into Aldolphina's eyes, Cyrill took the fruit and began to eat. The decree of the King stated "By agreement of two, a thing is established." The two children had established evil upon the earth.

Night had fallen upon the forest and never had the darkness been so thick. Always in the past the children had been able to see through the darkness of night. Tonight neither Cyrill nor Aldolphina could see into the forest. Neither child could see past the other. They clung together in loneliness. They were so alone.

Hiding in fear they felt confused. There was no expectation for what the outcome of their act would be because having experienced the unknown, the result was also unknown. Always before this moment they had felt in control of their past, present and future; now they had no idea where they were headed. The two children were lost and so they hid. They knew not what they were hiding from. The forest was not speaking and they were cold. Never before had they felt cold, why it was as if they had no covering.

Shivering the two children drew close together for warmth and comfort. New sensations began to take over their thoughts and their bodies. The touch of their skin sent strange unfamiliar tingles up Cyrill's spine. Aldolphina felt her legs grow weak and the longing within her became overpowering. What happens next was a performance their young minds were not prepared for.

At that moment the two became one; one united against their King. The act clinched the separation of all mankind from the King. The act of multiplication fit into the King's purpose for the children but was to be performed in obedience and love, not out of fear and longing. The longing could never be satisfied by this act or any act, the longing was a sign of the separation from the King. It would remain for a long time.

The serpent had watched the entire event unfold with much glee. "What a splendid job. I could not have asked for better results. Now the King will throw them out and I will be waiting to catch them," he laughed so hard the forest trembled in trepidation

Another also watched the event. "Tomorrow I will go to them. I will not wait for them to come to me. I will go to my precious children." Although the King had the remedy in place to help His children, it also hurt Him. Because as King, He would have to follow the law He put in place. There was a required punishment for this willful act of disobedience and he would endure separation from them for a time. But he would never take his eyes off them until they were once more one with him.

The King had established the principles not with discipline of the children in mind, but to ensure the uniform function of the earth he created for his children. So long as the children complied with the King's instructions to obey and love; the principle of rewards to compliance was in effect empowering the children to prosper by the work of their hands and the children were in spiritual union with the King.

The only one who could cause change to this unity was the children of the King. The King would not cause change because His word was the law. He could not go back on his word. He was sworn to never leave or abandon his children.

Now His beloved Cyrill and Aldophina had put the earth in a state of lawlessness, and because of their rebellion all man-children were now in a state of anarchy. The King's thoughts were rapidly spinning in the spirit realm. "They did not understand they had initiated a separation between him and all man-children. Cyrill had sealed the separation when he chose Aldophina's word over Royal instructions. They have placed themselves outside realm of truth by letting fear in and into the realm of darkness. The Spirit he had placed in each of the children could not mix with darkness any more than fear could mix with truth. The King's Spirit given the children began to recede as their fear grew. "Didn't the children know how much He loved them? He would never leave them to solve their problems alone. Even if they were at fault, they were His children and He would protect them. But would they trust him enough to be honest?"

"Because of the children's disobedience the entire declaration of the King's principles and laws governing the earth were now in rebellion also. The ground would no longer obey the command of the children. The ground was obligated to obey only those children in right standing with the King's laws.

The same was true of the animals. Soon the children would no longer be able to communicate with the animals. For this reason immediately the large dinosaurs began to die. The King had to remove them from among the children. They too now sought to exert dominance over their ruler, the man-child. Just as the man-child had rejected the commands of his creator, the King; now all things created by the King for the man-child rejected the commands of the man-child."

Only when the man-child was brought back into unity with the King, would the principles and laws governing creation return to right standing. Two things are required here thought the King. "The required penalty must be paid and since evil was established by the agreement of two; each child would be required to accept the remedy to be reunited to the King for him or herself."

"But my beloved children will stay in a separated state until the penalty for their crimes are satisfied. The internal spirit I have placed within each of them will continue to fade until it is overcome by the realm of darkness and death. This means that not only those here now, but all those who will come later will be subjected to the rule of darkness. When my power fades inside of them, they will be helpless, even if they try to resist evil."

"They have traded the Royal covering for a coat of blame. I must put my Royal dressing back on them as only I can. But I can have no part with them in their present condition and they are condemned by their actions. They require immunity for their crimes against the Kingdom." At that time the King dispatched orders for the helpers to be on standby to prepare a Royal garment that would be made of invincible sacrificed blood.

"To receive protection the Kingdom will have to make a convent with them, but the situation requires an advocate since I myself cannot represent them in their present condition. A good advocate can plead their case for immunity and insure the penalty is paid. The law requires death as payment for their disobedience. I cannot break the law. Living in a separated state from me their spirit will continue to die. Because they choose the voice of evil, their flesh will be under the control of evil for so long as they are alive." The King knew the only solution was for one great enough to satisfy the law of death for all the children at one time. The only one great enough for such a thing was He.

"Just cause must support restoration of the connection between the children and me. In this way their spirits may live. The only way to save their spirits is for a substitute to receive the penalty. They were unblemished and the substitution requires purity. This is the only means for immunity."

"It will require one with an untarnished mind and heart; who is able to live in the midst of the temptations present without disobeying the Kingdom rules. It will require love for the Kingdom and for the children."

"When the replacement is in place, the convent will require acceptance on behalf of the Kingdom and the guilty party if the payment is to be affirmed. Both parties must agree. Without acceptance on the part of the guilty party, the agreement will be invalid.

To bind them to me forever, I must do something that only I can do. The law requires the price of death to be paid. Immediately the King's Word and Spirit were in agreement with the thought of the King. The Word prepared to become personified into a male child and to be born of woman. The Spirit of the King prepared to insert the Word into the chosen body of the girl picked by the King. "These I will place in honor above all others," said the King.

"To accept the payment, the children will have to do what they did not do before. That means they will need to believe in me. They must know the contract with me is all that is needed for their continuance and joy. It will require confidence in my word. My word will always perform its' intended purpose. I can count on my word to perform everything I speak it for. It was my word which suffered the offense, but my word will now show ultimate love and forgiveness by paying the price of the offense."

"I will cause my Royal word to become Royal flesh just as I gave life to their bodies, I will give flesh life to my word. Royal flesh must redeem what was lost by Royal flesh. But now all flesh is no longer Royalty. Flesh bodies will die, but the Royal spirit of my word is forever. The Royal spirit of my word is love. Therefore the one embodied in my word will be love.

This one will draw them back to me and they will speak my words uniting our spirits once again. It will require trust in me to believe the spirit will return to me to live forever in my Kingdom. Once I have their trust we will be as one."

"No on can be coerced into this agreement, it must be believed willingly and only the spirit is covered by the contract. The flesh belongs to the earth realm and must return to the earth, but the spirit belongs to me and must return to me. Then the immunity of the Kingdom will be in place forever. I will show them mercy and we will be reunited forever."

"However none of these provisions will be established unless they testify in the earth and the heavenly courts of the Kingdom of the goodness of the Kingdom. They can only testify after admitting disobedience. By admitting disobedience they affirm my right to govern them according to my plans and purposes."

"With the mouth they must acknowledge the payment of Royal blood for their disobedience. They by their actions are no longer Royalty so Royalty will have to be provided. They must acknowledge the Royal word of the King became a son born through an earthly vessel to become flesh. Then and only then will I grant them immunity for all wrongs confessed."

All these thought speed through the King faster than the speed of light and just as like that the answer to the dilemma of saving the children was made ready. The answer was in the King's love.

Long before any of these things, the King had promised, "He would cause all things to work for the good of his children," and so there was also joy to be had. Aldolphina was with child. The child would a boy and his name would be called Christian. Christian would have a special job to undo what his earthly parents had done. But first the King needed to make the way for Christian to be successful.

CHAPTER FIVE

The Confrontation

Luke 10:18-20

And he said unto them, I beheld Satan as lightning fall from heaven.

Lucre continued with his plan; lying seeds of jealousy, fear and envy all along the trail of the journey. Feeling that he had accomplished his goal with Cyrill and Aldolphina, Lucre turned full attention to the other riders along the trail. Lucre whispered words of comfort that were meant to destroy the children. Lucre had learned many things from the King, but the most important thing he learned was the power of words.

Coming across Sharon, Lucre approached the shy young girl, "You are doing very well to be by yourself." "Thank you," the young girl said never raising her head. "Why are you alone?" Lucre knew the girl's shyness and decided to use it against her. "I really wanted to ask Charles to partner with me, but I have a problem speaking to others. Besides Charles so popular I'm sure he wouldn't partner with me," Sharon said. "I wish I could just speak up like others."

"Oh no Sharon, it's not you. It must be the way the King intended. Perhaps you don't speak up because it's a way of safety the King instilled in you. You know I heard Charles and some other boys laughing about your speech. If you had ask him, why he might have embarrassed you. Be glad the King gives you caution and continue on your own."

Feeling truly hurt and embarrassed Sharon stumbled down the path blinded by tears. When who should appear but Charles? Alarmed and distressed by Sharon's tears, Charles immediately raced to console her. Sharon was one of his favorite among the children.

Seeing Charles before her, Sharon blurted out mean hateful words to express all the hurt in her heart. She never considered the hurt was caused by Lucre's words which in turn controlled her thoughts. She spoke from her pain, not out of her spirit, but the words still had power.

When finished she ran away leaving the effects of her words with Charles. Stunned the boy felt crushed and confused. Two children had been hurt by Lucre's lie, but there was also evil let loose upon the trail by the words spoken. Words once spoken live on unless the speaker cancels the word.

Lucre understood that the King and his word were one and the same principle applied to the children created by the King. He knew there was no way to separate the speaker from the word. Whatever the children spoke is what they would become.

Lucre had to get the children to speak evil about each other and this place, but he really wanted them to speak bad things about the King. Because the children were inherently good, the only way to induce negative speech was to cause doubt. Doubt about the creation, doubt about each other and doubt about themselves would eventually lead to doubt about the King. He had to destroy their trust in the King if he was ever to become great.

Whenever his path crossed one or more of the children, Lucre created lie after lie to cause hurt. Where once he had been patient, he now grew very impatient. He wanted to be as great as the King and he wanted it now!

Lucre had a special reason for wanting to prove himself as strong as the King. Knowing he was not made of the King's spirit and the King had not breathed his life into him, Lucre was jealous of the children, so he determined that he would be King himself.

The children grabbed hold of the feelings of pain and hurt, ignoring the principle of love. It was as though they forgot all the principles the King had taught them.

Aldolphina and Cyrill were in hiding. The two had love for everyone including the King, but something was wrong. They had no idea the effect their disobedience had on the journey "Why were they so cold?" The children did not know a war had begun and the battle was well under way.

All around them the journey was becoming catastrophic for the children. But there was one who saw and knew all things. This same one had all the answers they needed, but first the children would have to seek His help.

The King came into the forest and began to call out for Cyrill and Aldolphina. Although both children heard the call, they were too scared to answer. Just as they tried to do things their own way before, now they were in disobedience again. Over and over the King had told them, "I have prepared the way for those I call." They doubted because of their own disobedience.

Patiently the King called, but no one, no not one of the children would heed his call. Finally the King went to them. "Where were you when I call?" "We were hiding because we were without your covering and we didn't want you to see," Cyrill said. The King looked at the children and spoke, "I would never take my covering from you. If you are without my covering, it's because you choose to go your way and leave my covering. I have you given you free will and of your will you have chosen to follow a way I did not make for you. Because of this your way will be hard. You will have many problems along the way you have chosen. But I will make the way for you to come back to me."

At that moment Lucre reared his ugly head. All pretense of love was gone. Immediately he began to speak words of accusations against the children. Although he had encouraged them to disobey, it was their choice to either obey Lucre's word or the Royal word. The King's word spoke of obedience to him and brought rewards, where as Lucre word spoke of disobedience to the King and brought curses with them. The children didn't understand. They thought they were choosing for themselves but they were being tricked into obeying Lucre.

Then he turned to the King and said, "You made the law and the punishment of the law. Are you going back on your word or will you punish the children according to your law. The result of disobedience is death." Standing there with evilness all over his face, Lucre waited for the King to answer.

Turning to the children, he stated, "Because of your actions you have entered into the phase of death. Decay and deterioration will be your future. It is the law. The penalty for your disobedience is death to your earth body. Death occurs when you are separated from my life source and places you into eternal darkness. Your relationship with me has been severed."

"Therefore your likeness to me, which is my spirit, has begun to die. Soon your earth body will cease to exist. The spirit needs the earth body to control the earth. So your spirit will depart the decayed earth body and live separated from me in darkness through out all eternity. You will be a weak tortured spirit without light. I must abide by my word and insist the price for this disobedience to be paid."

"There must be Royal blood to recompense the debt. Blood is the life source of your earth body and without it the earth body dies. But without Royal blood it can have no true life. Due to your disobedience death of the earth body is also required leaving your spirit without a home. The heart without Royal blood produces evil thoughts. The Royal law requires the debt be paid with Royal blood. I will honor my word when I said, "I will never leave you or abandon you.""

Hearing this Lucre again started to rant and rave for justice. "How can you stand by these you created? They are subject to the laws you created. Are you not righteous and truthful? They must be judged according to their choices." Lucre sought to trap the King by His own laws; he did not know the King had prepared the blood required for payment of the children's wrongs. But now it was time for Lucre to receive that which he cried for. Time was drawing near for Lucre to be punished and there would be no mercy from the King.

Just as the King reminded the children that true love calls for obedience, the same was true for Lucre. As the King said, "Disobedience for His rules would cause love for him to cease and without love for Him all love would cease, even love for self. At which point you began to self destruct." Lucre had begun to self destruct.

The King represents justice and justice sometimes requires punishment. But punishment alone is not complete justice. To be just, one must also be fair. A key part of justice is to allow everyone to have the freedom to choose.

Loving as He does, the King is never bond his love allows him total freedom to rule in righteousness. Having a lack of restrictions the King knows no temptation. There is no one higher than the King and his love protects all those below him if they will accept him without doubt. He is freedom.

This is the freedom the King desires for His children. The freedom of love. Love always requires submission. Therefore just as the children are required to submit to the established laws the King is also bond by His word to remain true to His law. That's why the King said, "If you love me, you will obey me." The King knew the power of love, because he was love.

Lucre saw this but he choose to lie rather than to submit to truth. Making his choice he set about to build a Kingdom based on lies. Doubt was the first step to get the children to believe a lie. Doubt suggested the King had lied leaving the children in search of something else to believe. The suggestion to doubt was enough to plant a seed. If not rejected by confronting the doubt with the truth of the King's word the seed would grow until the doubt had taken over the mind of the child. The only way to reject the seed was to believe the King and all that he had shown of Himself. To agree with the doubt was to agree with Lucre.

The King gave everyone free will to choose. Lucre chose to go against the King. Just as he demanded judgment for the children, he too would pay the price for his wrongs.

The King withdrew into His spirit kingdom with Lucre following close behind demanding judgment upon the children. Never ceasing to remind the King of the principles He established for creation to continue and flourish, Lucre stayed in the King's court hurling accusations of disobedience toward the children. "Guilty! Guilty!" he yelled all day in regards to the children. Constantly he demanded payment be made for the children's disobedience.

When he wasn't accusing the children to the King, he would whisper accusations to the children to remind them of how imperfect they were. After all with so many imperfections, how could they believe they were Royalty? In this way Lucre weakens the children's believeth in the King based on how they felt about themselves.

When the King had let Lucre speak for some time he answered him. "Every punishment you have demanded of my children you will receive. As you have judged so shall you be judged. You demand that I throw them out of the garden; you are to be thrown out of my kingdom. You demand their way to be hard and unproductive; your way will be unproductive. You demand punishment; well I have prepared a place for you and all the helpers who followed you. In a short while you will go there and be punished for all eternity but first you will help my children to regain favor."

Looking flabbergasted, and fearing that he had gone too far; Lucre said in a timid voice, "How can I or anyone help them regain favor?" Trying to buy time with the question, Lucre was searching his dark thoughts looking for a way to still have the kingdom he desired. Seeing no way out of the corner he was in, he signaled for his band of followers to join him in war against the King. This was a private signal he had worked out earlier in case it came to this. But the King knows all things.

Not waiting for the answer to his question, Lucre and his band attempted to overthrow the King. Of course the King was prepared and expecting the assault. It was for this reason the King had retired to the spirit kingdom when Lucre pursued him. The King knew that to do battle on the earth would destroy it. He moved the battle away from the children into the spirit realm. This battle was His.

The King raised his right hand and lighting so hot no man or beast could have withstood it flashed across the heavens. Thunder with a magnitude of noise beyond the human ability to tolerate bounced through out heaven. The echo could be heard through out the forest and all creation scattered to hide from the King's wrath.

Lucre and his band found themselves being beaten and tossed from one end of heaven to the other. They splatter like eggs when stepped on. Their beautiful shapes were changing with each blow until they were all horribly misshapen and grotesque in form.

The entire time the King had only to keep his right hand raised in righteousness. Never did He raise a finger to touch the horrible helpers. His command was His weapon and all elements obeyed. The beating went on for quite some time and then the King lowered his hand swiftly and just like that Lucre and all his followers hit the earth with such ferocity a great tear was left in the ground.

The King filled the cavern with fire and chains to be used to bound the rebellious helpers. "Lucre as I said, you have a short time in which you will be instrumental in helping my children regain favor. After that time you will be bound in this place for all eternity. As of this moment you are stripped of all power in heaven and on earth. I leave you with only your lies to war with."

Confused and not understanding what the King meant by "Helping the children regain favor," the beaten helper cowered to the dark recesses of the earth. Here the King had banished him and all his followers until that final Day of Judgment. "They would forever reside in darkness, never to enjoy the warmth of the King's light again."

The King removed all resemblance of human appearance from them when He stripped their power. The only form they possessed mirrored their spirits; they were dark and ugly forms. Although they could no longer transform into human appearance of their own, they were able to become invisible to the children. But much more dangerous was their ability to enter into the human form of the children, if the children invited them in. This was because of the freedom to choose the King had bestowed upon his children.

While the King was thrashing Lucre and his band in the spirit world; the children's activities was becoming increasingly more difficult to accomplish. There was mistrust among the children and they no longer combine forces to achieve the desired goals. As their inner spirits grew dim, they were lacking in wisdom. Not understanding the changes happening all around as well as within, the children struggled to make it to the finish line hoping to go home to Eden but no one knew the way home. Most were not aware the garden had been shut to them until such a time when they returned to right standing with the King.

It was in this atmosphere the unknown child appeared. No one could remember seeing this child before. The boy was not particularly beautiful but there was an aurora of beauty all about him. He always appeared along the journey with words of encouragement reminding the children how much the King loved them.

The King had been mindful of the condition of his children all the while Lucre was bringing their disobedience to his court. Being King, he was not going to leave His children without a way out. "What kind of father would desert his children when they needed him most," He said to Lucre. But Lucre knew the King would not violate His own laws so he felt certain he had won and the King would have to turn His back on the Children. Then Lucre could use them to build his kingdom.

The King had a plan. The character of a King or a man cannot exceed the value of his word and his substance. The King's substance is love. Because He is completely spirit; love is his heart and life force. It was this love which made Him intent on saving His children. It was love that inspired the King to choose a special role for Christian in His plan to save the children.

The King would clothe his word in human form giving earthly life to his life force of love. The word wrapped in earthly life would contain the life force of blood. Because blood was required for life on earth, it would require the pouring out of blood to save the children. Without blood the human form would die. Death was the requirement for disobedience and rebellion to the decrees of the kingdom. So the word whose essence was love became human to die in place of the children.

The King's love was as much a part of the King as His word. That's because the King's Spirit is love. The Spirit and the word were part of the King from the beginning. Just as all things were made of His word, all things were made out of His love.

The word would cause the Spirit to move into action and creation would take place. Therefore the King's son was before all creation and before all man-children. There was no way the children could know him because he was before the beginning of their knowledge. However they too had the same spirit before disobedience occurred.

By now many of the children were feeling the effects of disobedience. As a result of their actions they were also in much doubt about the King. The children never realized it was their disobedience breeding distrust in their hearts. The King had not changed, they had changed.

After some time Aldolphina give birth to the child conceived by her and Cyrill. The baby was called Christian. Immediately the unknown child began to look after young Christian. He nourished the baby with many good things. The food he feed the child with was the bread of life.

As soon as the baby could speak, the unknown child filled his head with words. Not just any words, but the word of the King. Everything created came from words and if the child was to create good things, he needed good words. So the unknown child filled young Christian's mind with thoughts of the King. Only the King was good.

Seeing the love the unknown child showed to her baby, Aldolphina felt regret at her own betrayal of the King. How she longed to make it up to the King. By now she knew her disobedience had been a betrayal to the King, but she also understood the word spoken in sincerity could change things. For this reason she was grateful to the unknown child. He was teaching her son the power of words.

Christian grew in strength and wisdom; regaining some of the mastery his parents had once had over the forest. The unknown child taught Christian in the power of believing what things he desired. He taught Christian the words and principles of the King.

For many days Christian was disciplined in the knowledge of the King under the teachings of the unknown child. The unknown child told Christian, "To know the King is to know the way of life." How the young child sucked up all knowledge introduced to him by the unknown child. Christian progressed fast and before long he was sharing his new knowledge with his mom and others.

Adolphina and Cyrill longed for the days when they were filled with excitement in knowing the King. That was before they were separated from him. Now it was all they could hope to get a glimpse of Him as He passed. No longer did they feel at one with their beloved King.

This made the unknown child very important to Aldolphina. She knew He gave Christian the one thing she could not. Through him, Christian knew the King, for this she would be forever grateful. Although time had passed she continued to blame herself for the King's absence.

The unknown child would cause crowds to gather when He began to teach on the King. It was not planned; there was a longing for the King. All the children like Cyrill and Aldolphina missed the King and wanted to hear from Him. Unable to hear from Him directly, they sought out this strange new child who had intimate knowledge of their beloved King.

Therefore soon after the teaching started, a large crowd would encircle the unknown child to hear his message. It was at a gathering like this the crowd became hungry. Now the unknown child had other followers beside Christian. Christian was the youngest. The followers suggested the crowd break and go home to eat.

This was an opportunity to show the King's strength. The unknown child wanted only to draw the children back to the King. So he instructed his followers to use the power given by the King to provide food for the crowd. Not understanding what he meant, they looked to him bewildered.

"Is there not food here for the crowd?" he asks. After polling the crowd his followers found only the lunch of one little boy. The unknown child called for the lunch.

After giving thanks for the food, he envision in his mind all the people being feed and just as he envisioned in his mind, the small lunch supplied food for all.

Amazed by the amount of food which never ran out, his followers ask, "What magic has produced such results?" Looking at the group, the unknown child admonished his followers for not believing. "The King is all powerful and has no need for magic. If you would believe in who your father is and that he will provide all things for you, then you too will produce occurrences like this and even greater ones."

Although many of the children were amazed at the phenomenon; it was then that some became jealous of the unknown child. There was a small gang of children trying very hard to win the King over. The only problem was they tried please the King their way. This way of thinking had led to problems on the journey.

To these the unknown child was a threat. He had what they had lost. He had closeness with the King they desired. Out of resentment and bitterness the group gathered to plot against the unknown child.

Drawing him away while the others eat, the boys began to hit the unknown child with stones, knives and sticks. All the while beating him they hurled untrue accusations upon the boy. Repeating the lies they learned from Lucre. There was great pain inflicted upon the boy's body, but he never cried out in pain. Jealousy had taken hold of the gang as over and over they brutally tore into his body. Backing up the child found himself backed to a tree. It was then the point the spear was thrust through his heart and his blood splattered the earth.

During this gathering the King was present listening to the hearts of His children. This night the King would be reunited with those whose heart longed for him.

The mood had become festive with the serving of food and many in the crowd were singing the old songs praising the King. It had been so long since they had felt light hearted and free. However within the crowd there were some whose hearts were being lead by Lucre. Lucre and all his followers mingled unseen within the crowd. Since he and his band had been banished to darkness, they were no longer seen, but they could be heard. They tried to disguise their words to sound like the King and in this way they deceived many of the children.

Most of their time was spent identifying the children who had lost hope. These they would convince to follow them. Carefully they chose the words that would help them accomplish their goals. Telling the hopeless children, "The King will never come again. Join us. We have a beautiful kingdom where there are no rules." But tonight they had another objective.

On this night they incited jealousy and envy toward the unknown child. As the party mood wore on, the feelings of jealousy increased. Lucre could be heard saying, "Who does he think he is? Are not all children as important as him?" Lucre always supplied questions, but never answers.

The children thought the questions were from other children, but no one stepped up to defend the unknown the child who was now missing from the crowd. Lucre always sneaks in unnoticed. The King had warned the children to be aware but they forgot.

On the surface there was laughter in the garden as the children finished the evening meal. The awesome wonder and amazement generated by the miraculous meal could be felt by everyone. The event produced joy as though everyone present had been a part of a magnificent deed. In the early days it would be no wonder for the King to provide a meal for the children; it would not have caused a stir. But since the battle with Lucre began, things did not come as easy anymore. It required hard work to get the ground to produce wheat for food. The fact that the unknown child could produce such great results was evidence he knew the King very well.

The earth too seemed more beautiful tonight. The beautiful sun was a golden orange and sinking behind the mountains, while the moon rose with splendor and grace above the garden. All the stars were twinkling and seemed to smile down on the happy gathering. Music and song filled the air. There had not been so much joy and happiness in the children's home in long time.

Aldolphina enjoyed the festivities while keeping her eyes on Christian. Her boy had started life out in a way that neither she nor the King ever intended. Strange how something started in wrong had become something so beautiful. Christian had given her an insight into love she had never known before. The love for the King would always be s first in her heart, but somehow the way in which this child had been birth through her body made her love strong and different. There had been so much pain when the child entered the earth and this pain made him her possession. Remembering the searing hot pain as it bore its way through her body made her tremble even today. Nothing could have prepared her for that white hot pain and the way her blood poured from her body. It had been through the outpouring blood that her son emerged head first. His body being vulnerable was compelled to follow the head. As soon as the weak body cleared the passage way into the world, Christian made his presence known by opening his mouth and making screaming sounds. The screams sounded like the roar of a loud to her ears.

Years later as he grew long and lanky she had laughed with Cyrill that His body was His Achilles' heel. Cyrill had laughed back, "He'll have to protect His body but if he's ever hurt at least it will only be the heel; His strength is in His head." The two often shared the joke as the little boy grew in size.

Still had she not paid a price for him? Having suffered to give him life gave her ownership; she was responsible for him and she would protect him with her very life.

Now he had found acceptance and love from this new and strange child. In Aldolphina's mind the child could not possible know how her heart felt to see her baby accepted by him. Aldolphina had no idea how great a love this unknown child felt not only for her son but for all the King's children. He knew her sufferings to give birth but he too was prepared to pay a price to give life to the children. This child knew all things.

At that moment the thought of the unknown child crossed her mind and she looked around the crowd for him. Searching the crowd she did not see him.

The love inside her for the unknown child was equal to the love she had for her child because the unknown child so clearly loved Christian without thought of his beginnings. She always thought others would judge him because of the way he started life. But not only had the unknown child shown great love and care for her child, she felt certain it was because of his presence that she could now reach out to renew her closeness with the King. The love of this unknown child had given her renewed hope to find that which she had lost. Words of truth were spoken by the unknown child and they reached into her heart. But more than anything He inspired confidence in her place with the King, she was sure love was the answer to all her problems.

Expecting Cyrill to come any second anticipation grew inside of her. This morning while in meditation in the meadows, the love she felt made her speak to the King in silence as she always did. But because of the teachings of the unknown child she felt a strong conviction the King would come to her again.

She had started by thanking the King for His love and asking forgiveness. The words were simple but true. "I am sorry for not trusting you my Lord," she said.

"My King please forgave my act of disobedience. I willingly betrayed your trust. I also caused another to stumble by encouraging Cyrill to follow me. As though that was not enough, I caused shame upon an innocent unborn baby. You have given the baby I cherish total acceptance and granted him knowledge of you through the unknown child."

"You did not withhold yourself from my child because of me. Your greatness could not be limited my actions. This unknown child has shown my child as much love as you showed for each of us. You have allowed that he should grow in knowledge and wisdom of the Kingdom although he has never been there. He has exceeded men far above his age. All this you did because you are faithful, even after I betrayed you."

"I know now that nothing will cause you to stop loving your children. Just as I love the child you give me; you also love your children. Please come to Cyrill and myself in the garden during the cool of evening as before, that we may serve you royally forever."

Remembering that the King reads hearts, she knew the King heard the truth of her heart felt request. She ask the King to come and visit her and Cyrill tonight. Speaking from her heart the truth of her words rang out. She knew the King would acknowledge her request. Both she and Cyrill were filled with expectant excitement. She did so want to be rejoined with the King.

Cyrill was so excited. He loved to play for the King. Tonight he was going to play a new song for the King, one he had written special. Aldolphina glanced toward the forest expecting Cyrill to come running. Although she could not see the King, for the first time in a long time she felt His presence near.

Suddenly there was an eerie loud wail. At the same time there was blackness. It was unlike anything ever seen or felt in the Kingdom. The sound was sharper than the wind in the tallest trees tops and it pierced right into the heart. Everyone and everything stopped, frozen where they stood. There was a new and strange feeling in the air. The children did not like the feeling. The hair stood on the back of their necks; this did not feel good. Could someone make it go away? The sound echoed and bounced off the trees, off the mountains and the wailing was going on forever.

Later, much later the children found out the name for the strange new ugly sensation. The name was grief; one of many new emotions they had come across since they separated from the King. The sensation of grief was often accompanied by the wailing sound. The King had never intended for the children to experience the sensation or the results associated with the word. Right at this moment, they wanted to get away from the sound and the feeling that was with the sound. The problem was they were unable to move and unable to speak. So everyone stood glued to the ground and the sound went on and on melting into the hearts of all who heard it.

Then Maylene and Michael, two of the King's faithful helpers appeared overhead. The helpers seldom used their wings, because they preferred to appear in form as the children. But now they flew out with golden wings a flutter and it was not until then that the children realized the loud wailing was coming from the earth. Round and round Maylene and Michael flew overhead. The wailing continued all the while.

The two carried something between them, but it was impossible to tell what it was because of the speed in the fluttering of their wings. The golden wings fluttered fast and furious beating out a strong wind. The wind was pushing the children off their feet. Maylene and Michael were barely more than a blur. There was no chance to see the object between them.

Then the King's voice was heard booming like thunder. Never had they heard the King's voice in that tone. Loud and deep the King's voice seems to come from the center of the earth and the heavens all at the same time. Then out of no where a bright spotlight shone on the form of the unknown child. He was impaled by a spear through his heart upon the tree he had stood beneath.

Before the interruption everyone had been eating and had not seen the attack upon him. But there on the ground beneath the tree, gleaming in a light that came from high above was His blood. The blood had a life of its own and radiated light. Someone had put a knife into the innocent child's heart. There was agony and pain on his twisted face but he did not appear surprised. His eyes looked toward the sky as his life's blood ran into the earth. The very earth the children were a part of.

The wailing stopped. Maylene and Michael lowered themselves to the ground and stationed in front of the unknown child as if to guard His body. The spirit within the body strained for release. This spirit was headed for eternal darkness in payment for the law the children had broken. Doomed to forever seek truth and light but condemned to darkness to repay that which was owed by others. The King himself had provided the payment to save his beloved children by causing his word to become flesh and take their place.

The rumbling of the King's voice could be heard to say, "This was my son. Sent to right the wrongs committed by his brothers." The children were afraid and whenever they were frightened, they hid from the King.

For many days now they had each longed for the King. Now they were afraid to go to him. Never had they heard the King sound like this! In an instant the children and the followers of the unknown child all ran for cover. Aldolphina had run to Christian attempting to snatch the boy from harms way, but the little boy stood rooted to the spot watching his teacher. The blood of the unknown child had spattered Christian the moment his heart was pierced. Christian and His mother had rounded the corner at the moment of impact. No amount of force could pull him away.

Maylene and Michael stood before the unknown child shielding his bleeding body from farther harm. There were low, mournful sounds coming from each of them. They sounded like two doves.

The unknown child slumped lifeless while the two looked after his spirit which was posed to leave the earth body.

Maylene and Michael knew this spirit wouldn't return to the King until control of the children was relinquished from Lucre. They stayed with the body of the earth child. After some time his spirit shining bright as gold exited the bruised body and entered a cage made of light carried between the two helpers. Yes this spirit would meet the requirement to enter eternal darkness, but this spirit would enter encased in the light of the King. This spirit would overcome the darkness with the King's light. This spirit would never be doomed to wonder in darkness forever. This spirit would not only overcome the requirement of darkness, but would shed light into the darkest regions forever. The price would be paid but the victory would belong to the unknown child.

The words, 'It is complete' resonate through out the land; traveling without end. Then King released Maylene and Michael and they flew away taking the unknown child's spirit with them. The two escorted the lighted spirit to a world of darkness to defeat all powers of the darkness forevermore. Never would the children need pay the price of separation from the King again.

High above from His throne, the thunderous voice of the King rumbled once again. The King instructed the children to come from hiding. There was silence and no one moved. Again the King called. This time the thunder was much louder causing a rumbling within the ground which threatens to crumble the earth. The children trembled and cried in the shadows afraid to cry out loud.

Finally a small voice answered the King's thunder. "Father we are not adorned in the dress of Your Royal Highness. We bring shame as we are. The covering we wear is spoiled and dirty. We are ashamed for you to see us like this. Our hearts grieve for the way we were before. Please don't look at us Father."

"Aldophina this day you spoke with conviction in heart and requested my presence. I am here just as you requested. Tell me what has happen to your princely array? Why is your dress in unbefitting children of the King?" At last Aldolphina crept from her hiding place. Filled with guilt and the new sensation of grief, Aldolphina looked at the lifeless body and cried for the undeserved death of a boy who shared love with all. The tears rushed uncontrollably from her eyes.

"Father ever since Lucre was helping me with a problem I had with Cyrill everything changed. I first disobeyed your instructions. Afterwards I experienced feeling badness, but not before I convinced Cyrill to disobey you also. I never came to you seeking your help and now tonight looking at the body of that poor dead boy, I feel totally exposed to all, without protection. As if everyone knows how horrible I am. I feel vulnerable to all manner of things. I have no shield from danger."

The King looked at Aldolphina and then he looked at the body. Softly he said to her, "Do you know why this innocent child gave his life in this manner?" Answering him, she turned her tear stained face up, "He did not give his life; it was brutally taken. I know now what death is because I feel it in my body."

The King looked on the girl with love saying, "Do you know how much he loved you? To love and teach love was his passion. It was out of love that he gave his life. Yes, he gave his life for your life. Does not my word teach you to love and protect your brother? This one was my word and all that it stands for.

"The authority of my word to act on your behalf was handed over by you to Lucre by your actions. My word was birth through an earth body to regain that which belonged to me before an earth body carelessly gave it away. The power of my word has now been restored to balance."

"You and the others made what you thought were innocent choices, but they were choices made without my guidance. You did not come to me for help. Did I not tell you to give me all your concerns? I am your provider. It is not my will to control you. That is why I did not speak you and the others into existence. If I had spoken you into existence as I did all other things you would be forced to do exactly as I spoke you. It was never my intention to control you, but to love you and to watch you grow in love from my teachings. True love grows from freedom, but real freedom comes from putting others first. Your needs and desires are my first concern and I will not seek harm for you."

"That also means I will provide answers for your problems. I created all things. Do you think I only provide the things seen? No I also provide things that are unseen. I've told you to never rely solely on your own understanding. I've been right here waiting for you to come to me yet only the death of one child and the love for your child moved you to seek me. Do you not know how much I love my children?"

"Was it pride that made you look for answers on your own?" "Aldolphina you and all the others have only one thing to be prideful of and that is that you are my children, the King's children. Even in that you must remember that it was I who made you, so the pride is mine, not yours."

"You and the others disobeyed me and cause a separation between us. The separation resulted in your nakedness because I had to remove my covering from over you. Nakedness, grief and death, these things I never told you of and you now know of them only because you disobeyed. They are emotional fruits grown from evil seeds. I never wanted you to know of evil. There was no need because evil could not touch you so long as you choose my way. But you choose another way. By choosing another way you have allowed evil seeds to take root in your mind. Once the mind is contaminated, it must be renewed, but I will take care of that."

"You must believe me if your mind is to be renewed. False thoughts and teachings will arise from those who mean you harm causing darkness in your mind. Trust me and I will guide your steps when the path becomes treacherous. My words will light the path for you to follow. I can only guide you so far as you obey me and you can't obey me unless you trust me. Trust means not trying to do it your own way, let me lead you please. I will even hold your hand all along the way when we travel. Do you understand Aldolphina? You will always have questions and problems, but it's ok. If you never had problems, you would never need me and I could never show you how much I love you, my dear girl. I promise I will be with you in times of trouble just I am in good times. I will not change."

Aldolphina lay like a withered flower. Sobs racked her body and even her bones felt dry and stuck to her skin. The feeling inside Aldolphina could not be described. Her body felt weak, limp and there was a great dry lump where her heart should been have. The pain ran through her body. "How can you speak of love when the destruction I caused stares at you?" Emotions of guilt and self-condemnation were overcoming the girl. Weak with grief, sorrow, guilt and shame, she longed to feel the King's arms around her. How she needed Him, there was no one else who could comfort her.

Yet all these new emotions stood between her and where the king sat on his throne. The feelings inside of her would not allow her to run to her Father for comfort, but she couldn't stay where she was. The emotion of guilt pressed down on her making her unable to move. How could he possible love her after what she had done? The King was to be to be feared and at this moment she knew his greatness like never before. She was thinking, "At a time when anger could be used, he is controlled by love for His children"

In a long pause of silence, Aldolphina blamed herself for what had happen to the precious child. The King waited, looking at the broken girl. The bright red circle of blood was ever present to the King as though the unknown child himself stood between the two.

Then Christian walked up to his mother and spoke, "Why are you sad? He promised He would return." The words spoken out the mouth of her baby sounded of truth although she had never heard the unknown child speak the words. Aldolphina didn't know why Christian spoke these words, but she knew they were true. The hope she had at the beginning of the night returned to her heart with a violent force and deep in the bottom of her stomach she had peace.

The King's peace caused Aldolphina to call his name out of love for her. Softly, barely above a whisper, Aldolphina said the King's name. The word "Father" was barely a whisper. She felt for certain that he could not possibly hear her, it was only a whisper, but suddenly his hand was on her shoulder. Aldolphina could not possibly know how much it meant to the King to hear her call him "Father." Not waiting for her to come to him; he reached through the blood of the unknown child to Aldolphina. Aldolphina felt the blood had cleansed her. She responded with hope and thankfulness for the unknown child and his violent death which she was certain would correct her wrongs. The King had once again touched her and it had been so long since she last felt his touch. But with his touch peace flooded her entire being.

With the touch of the King, her clothes were transformed into Queenly garments. "I'm here," he said. Aldolphina could hardly believe her ears, surely she was mistaken, but her heart confirmed what she heard. Her heart confirmed her Father's voice. In that moment a vital truth was revealed in her heart. No emotion could change the King's love for her and if His love was unchanged, she knew His promises to her were unchanged. The King spoke to her with the love he had spoken before all these terrible things happen. Not the anger that his voice held when it rolled like thunder, but the love his voice held when he made the rainbow across the heavens for his children.

Slowly the frighten girl raised her head and grabbed hold of her King; at that moment all fear faded away. Relief flooded out of her tears as she put into words the emotions that were in her heart, the desire for forgiveness. As soon as the words were out of her mouth, the King forgave her. "I heard you ask with your heart and now that you've spoken the words, I am glad to give you what you ask for. We will put this behind us and never mention it again."

"Come there is much work to be done. We must save your brothers and sisters. Now go and get them.

Aldolphina felt real freedom since the first time when Lucre had offered to help her. No more secrets, the King knew all and he still loved her. Although she didn't know how it would happen, Aldolphina knew the King would work everything out and in the strangest way, she felt the King would make things right for the unknown child also. It would be three days before Christian saw the unknown child.

When Lucre saw the unknown child dead, he was excited and panicky at the same time. That idiot Cannon had really let jealousy get the better of him. Cannon lay twisting in torment over the wrong he had done. Lucre stormed in and screamed at Cannon, "Stand up you fool!" There was no need to be gentle, he was finished with him. So he increased the torment of words meant to produce guilt and shame until he drove Cannon mad. Then in one swift blow, after killing the unknown child, Cannon drew his own blood and died.

He had not convinced as many to join him as he wanted, but no matter, it would be enough for now. Besides the King would have to punish the others by throwing them out of the Kingdom, wouldn't he? Where else could they go? They would need him now. Lucre felt wild with excitement, he was to finally have his Kingdom. Lucre was so deep in the darkness that he knew nothing about the light of the King.

Now that that idiot was out of the way, Lucre had to gather his followers. Together they would get to the children while they were afraid. As long as they had fear, they would be easier to lead. He just needed to use the fear to convince them that the King didn't love them.

But once again Lucre misjudged the power of the King's love for his children. What they could not do for themselves, the King could through grace. It was possible to show grace because he could now grant immunity to His children. He would provide them with strength until all were taught in the way of immunity.

The work he had begun; he would not let a foolish, evil helper like Lucre destroy. The King's desire was for all to be saved. But none of these things did Lucre know.

Lucre gathered his followers and ran out unseen among the children. "Go quickly and find the children while their fear is high! The moment had arrived for his triumph. It will be hard for the children to hear the King even if he calls; their fear will block his voice. The King's words cannot penetrate a heart filled with fear!" "Strike while the fear is there. It will act as a boiling kettle in their gut and block all entrance into their hearts. Now go quickly and remember to speak softly, seductively, and sweetly. They must believe your words are the answer they want."

Lucre and his gang went to work spreading chaos and confusion over the land of the children. No on was spared. Hopelessness settled into the minds of the children as they ran for cover. Nothing they had experienced prepared them for this onslaught of danger. Royal thoughts and courage were replaced with unsure thoughts causing most to stumble as they tried to stand and walk. Superior confidence and feelings of security were rapidly being smothered out as though someone had covered a flame with a blanket. All that remained was the blinding smoke of doubt and the heavy felling of guilt.

Lucre and his followers spread out quickly. They warned the children of the King's anger and made sure the children were afraid of the King. The separation between King and beloved child grew as the children shrank back from the King's love out of fear.

Suddenly a dark luminous cloud appeared in the eastern sky. A voice like rolling thunder sounded from the cloud. Lightening bolts covered the entire sky, flashing from the south. Rolling gales of wind blew in gusts from the north. The sound of rolling thunder and loud rushing wind filled the air as powerful electric currents penetrated the air and crackled with big popping sounds. The entire atmosphere was in an uproar. There was no peace to be felt.

Lucre enjoyed the chaos. Surely he was getting close to exerting control over these silly children. He so desired to be King. Here was his chance. Soon they would be his subjects ready to bow down before him. In the midst of his wild thoughts the elements of the atmosphere caught Lucre and his entire gang up in a violent force lifting them high above the earth. No longer were they the hunters; in a split second they had become the prey and there was no mercy to be shown. Violent combat was unleashed on the evil gang.

This went on for three days prior to Christian seeing the unknown child again. Christian and many others mourned the unknown child, thinking they would never see him again. The sky above the earth was a furious battlefield and on the earth shrieks of terror could be heard. Occasionally looking up the children caught sight of Lucre or one of his followers tumbling around. But mostly the children stayed out of sight in hiding unsure of what would follow next.

On the third day at the hour of noon a great cloud appeared. The King was seated on the cloud and to his right set the unknown child with the golden spirit intact and shining. Songs of joy were replacing the sound of thunder in the air. The flashes of lighting receded to be replaced by helpers in white robes. Only Lucre and his band remained encased in ferocious winds suspended between earth and the heavens.

A voice coming from the center of the cloud proclaimed, "Fear the King, the hour for judgment has come!" With that a vicious red hot flame of lightening struck Lucre, tossing him over and over like a slip of paper blowing in the wind. Violent winds swept the ragged band of followers along the rugged tops of the mountains and back again. The riders on the cloud set majestically watching as Lucre and his followers yelled for mercy. The sky turned from black to gray, and then the Sun broke through the dimness dripping with blood.

Lucre looking ragged and torn was not to be silenced. Trying to catch a breath between the churning motions he called, "Wait as King you must also send the children who disobeyed your rules along with us!" Lucre was looking for anything he could bargain with. He desperately wanted to destroy the children. They were the Kings' and he desired to hurt the King.

"Lucre did you think I was unaware of your evil plot? I prepared the way of recovery for my children some time ago. As much as I love the children, my word must not ever be compromised. Every penalty I spoke for their disobedience has been fulfilled by my word. That which the word required, the word provided. But there is no redemption for you Lucre. From this day forward you cannot touch or enter their earth bodies."

Then the King turned his attention to the children with Lucre watching, he wanted Lucre to witness the love he had for His children. "All who will be part of my Kingdom come down and put on your new Royal garment. These garments are weaved of a special material made of the blood of the unknown child. For three days the Royal helpers have fashion special garments for all who will accept them. This Royal garment is yours for all eternity if you accept it. Admit your wrongs and testify that by putting on this garment woven from the blood of the unknown child you are now pure. Testify with your mouth and give evidence by your actions your belief, this garment frees you from all danger. Proclaim with your mouth that the blood of the unknown child purchased your Royal covering and promise to obey the law of love."

As the children put on the garments fashioned of the special material, they felt clean for the first time since the foolish games with Lucre had started. As each put on their gowns, the children testified to the ability of the garment to wipe away all uncleanness. Songs of joy and praises to the King were heard all over the Kingdom as all the children sang. The unknown child set at the right hand of the King looking on the events in love.

Lucre cringed in pain knowing that his own evil deed had thwarted his plan. So that's what the King had meant when he said, "He would help the children." The King had turned Lucre's evil plot to bring damnation upon the children by allowing the unknown child to pay the required price of death for the children. The punishment deserved by the children was placed upon the back of another. This unknown child must surely be directly from the King. How else could he have come back to life?

Suddenly without warning as though he had enough, the King struck a far mountain with a fierce lightening bolt. The bolt bore a huge opening straight into the mountain. Thick black smoke along with red and yellow flames leapt from the hole in the mountain. The tempest wind encasing Lucre and his followers spurned wildly churning the group like chopped meat. Then the tail of the wind churned the screaming insurgents into a deep abyss of the mountain. They continued to shriek as the hole closed in upon itself.

The King looked upon the children. They stared in wonder and amazement in the direction of the mountain unable to speak. Then with fear and trembling, all bowed low waiting for the King to speak. The King said, "Lucre's jealousy and hatred held you in bondage, but love has freed you today. Today marks the beginning of many struggles for you. This is only the first of many battles to come. You have taken a big step toward finishing the journey I sat before. But you must transcend the condition you have fallen into. This was not the position you were created for. So long as you accept my word as truth you will win. But those who will war against you are evil ones. They will have no pity upon you so the Kingdom must be secured by force. Therefore you will need conviction in my sovereignty and who I am. There will be no room for doubt. Trust and know that your enemies are my enemies. Those who would war against you; I will war against them. Speak my word always, no matter what the circumstances may look like. Believe and speak my word always. I am not a man that needs to lie and my word cannot be changed. I am assuring you of victory now so you need never fear. Just believe my word and trust me.

The King has never stopped teaching his word even to this day and ordinarily the story would end here. However truth is essential for a child of the King to live and now seeds of doubt had been planted through out the path of the children. Each encounter with these seeds of doubt caused a little bit of the children's spirits to separate from the King and to die. Soon the children would be in a complete state of death if they were not saved. To overcome the doubt would require help from the very one that doubted. How would the children ever regain the trust they needed to take hold of the victory the King had promised?

Christian would learn to destroy the seeds of doubt from the teachings of the unknown child. For the children of the King, only the words of the King can be considered as normal. Everything else must be considered as foreign and was to be rejected by the children. Words which produce thoughts different than the King's thoughts were abnormalities. These words could not move the King's Spirit to power because they did not originate from the King's thoughts. The Spirit would only agree with the King's thoughts.

Lucre and his kind strayed away from the purpose the King created them for. They were aberrations. They were irregularities and void of all truth. They had become lies.

Lucre chose to become the opposite of what he was created for. Instead of a helper he chose to be a destroyer, but only the King's plan and purpose can succeed because he is the originator of all.

Now back to our story

CHAPTER 6

Lucres Thief of the Children

And Christian

1 Th 4:6

6 Therefore, let us not sleep, as do others, but let us watch and be sober-minded

Many years passed. The King's love for his children never waivered and the teaching of- His instructions continued by way of the words spoken by the unknown child. Many who had known the unknown child believed his pronouncements of the King. In this way knowledge of the King slowly spread. However there was one big problem. Now that the children knew evil, it was very hard for them to believe.

Oh they believed the King and they believed his power. After all hadn't they seen it for themselves? But it was hard to believe that the King had forgiven them. Many even doubted He still loved them, so how could he forgive them and take them back just as the horrible things never happen? Doubt was growing deep into the children's mind. Doubt lead to the children trying to save themselves from the effects of evil as well as trying to make life good. So instead of relying on the Royal garments made especially for them from the blood of the unknown child, they tried to make things better through their own power. The trouble with that was once evil came in they had no power. They were no longer privileged to the King's power from His Spirit. The only way for them to have the authority and power of the King's Spirit was to put on the garment woven of the unknown child's blood. There was no other way.

Before the Kingdom had been a happy place and yes they were happy again, but there was something else present now. They didn't know what it was, but the King knew. The children doubted Him because they had not forgiven themselves. So they found it hard to accept the King's forgiveness. The children were under condemnation for them and judged each other.

Under those conditions love was one thing not present. Only with love could they fight fear and hopelessness. Without love doubt flourished in the hearts and minds of the children and doubt put distance between them and the King.

To regain closeness with the King it would be necessary for the children to understand the magnitude of the love he had for each of them. Letting go of the resistance they had would let the King's love in. Submission was required to counter-act the rebellion which had caused the separation in the first place. If they could ever understand the enormity of his love, they would open up the closed areas of their heart and let him in. The King would force His way into their hearts, he wanted to be invited in.

If the damage caused by Lucre was ever to be undone, it was so important for the children to trust the King. Without trust the King could not fight for them. You see He had given them free will and He could only do that which they believed Him for. Submission was a way of showing their trust for Him. The King would never force His way on anyone. Trust would produce the kind of closeness the King wanted for his family.

But they lacked trust in the King. For this reason the children sought to take care of themselves. There was not enough of the spirit at work inside of them to make right what they had made wrong. Only with submission to the King would the blood garment be taken up and the King could not give new life to dying spirits unless the blood garment was accepted. Even the dying weak spirits within the children long for that which was true. Without truth there was only darkness. Darkness would produce constant torture to the spirit of the King's children because they meant to live in light.

They tried to understand the King's thoughts based on their own thoughts. The children did not know it was impossible to know the King's thoughts based on what they could think or feel. Emotions could not change the spoken word of the King. The King's words are spoken in justice, not out of emotion. Justice produce joy and unlike emotions joy did not change. Joy was the fiber used by the King to create.

Like the King himself, his thoughts and feelings were so much bigger and stronger than the children's. It was impossible to know just how strong, without his help. No one could know the King unless he allowed them to.

Knowing the thoughts of the children, the King worked very hard to show them how much he loved them. He did amazing miracles. One time the King made the Sun stand still for a long time, just because one of the children ask him to. Stopping time not only showed His love, but demonstrated the power of the children over time itself. Another time he made food fall from the sky so that the children didn't have to hunt or cook. The King tried hard to show the children there was no need to ever doubt him.

But with every doubt there was an act of disobedience and every act of disobedience created another evil. Then the evil would cause more condemnation and on and on the cycle went. After Lucre, there were so many problems. The children became confused and did not seek the King for help. However the King was always ready with an answer. If only they would ask. Still the King stayed near His beloved children.

While the King was trying to rebuild the relationship with the children, Lucre was busy trying to build a Kingdom. All the confusion and doubt served his purpose well.

Lucre foamed and raged after the battle between him and the King. He rallied his gang and began to tell of his plan. Didn't he know all the King's words? Sure this hole in the side of a mountain wasn't the beautiful garden on the other side, but he knew the secret to build it. Unlike those silly children of the Kings' he had listen to all the King's teachings. He had memorized every word. He could recite the King's lessons backwards and forwards. The King had gifted him, Lucre with the ability to anticipate the kid's needs before they ever put them into word. That was something

Lucre would need to train his team on. He never cared about their silly needs, but the silly children were always happy to think he cared. Oh no! He wasn't done with those ridiculous children yet. "I will have my Kingdom and they will help to build it! If not I will cause the destruction of every one of them."

Then he set to work creating his Kingdom. He would show them; anything the King could do, he would do also. Lucre set about gathering dirt and water. These were the materials the King used to create and fashion his children. Lucre set out to make animals and birds using the dirt and water.

Lucre had always been a good imitator and he called his trade, "magic." Lucre could copy the outward appearance of almost anything. So it was little surprise that the animals and birds looked very real. Only they were all in black and gray. Lucre also had problems making colors, so there was no color to be had in this place at this time. Only various shades of black and gray existed here. Even the mud was gray. Lucre was a master at illusion and making things appear to be real. The animals and birds set there looking real, but they were unable to make sound or to move. In short, they had no life in them.

The imitations needed life, but how would he give them life? "Bird fly," he commanded. Nothing happen. "Bird sing," he commanded in a louder voice. Nothing happen. Over and over he gave commands and made demands but could produce no life. Lucre worked for many days trying everything he knew. Breathing into the animals, he blew so hard they fell over. Not one mouthful of air came from the empty forms. Well he decided he would come back to the animals later.

Next he fashioned a tree. Surely this would be easier. After all the tree didn't have to make sound or breathe. "Trees only stand there and look pretty. I'm sure I can make pretty things," he encouraged himself. So Lucre went to work and took quite some time to finally get a large tree setting up. Unfortunately without life in it the tree could not produce pretty green leaves. Lucre hadn't thought of that. One could see Lucre's strange little crooked shape hoping around at a fast pace. In his anger his little contorted body changing quite rapidly. Quite a pity it was, Lucre had been the most beautiful of all helpers before his big blunder, now daily his form grew more grotesque.

His misshapen body resembled the sparse limbs of the trees he tried to make. The trees were without life just as his entire world was. Much time had passed since he had been kicked out of the Kingdom and he was becoming very frustrated with his progress. He needed to get his Kingdom ready to persuade the children to come over. Again trying to encourage himself he thought, "The children will bring color into this drab place. I only need to persuade them to come."

Lucre didn't really understand why his made up animals and trees weren't working, but he felt certain having the children here would make everything better. The King had spoke and made trees, streams, flowers and grass. Maybe it wasn't working for him, but the children were made like the King, they would be able to help.

For many days Lucre continued trying to apply the King's teachings to the black earth, but nothing was working. Finally Lucre realizes his words had no creative power. He could not give life and without life there was no creation. All he could do was to make empty lifeless imitations. If he was to be King, it would be King over the lifeless.

Slowly it was dawning on Lucre, "The Kings gifts and wisdom only work when used for the King's purpose and the King's purpose was for all creation to serve His children." Knowing the King wanted His children to prosper by growing in wisdom and love Lucre felt certain the children were key to his success. After all the King in His wisdom had supplied everything the children would ever need. The only thing the King required was for the children to rely on Him and Him alone.

Force to admit he did not have the gifts or power given the King's children, Lucre could be heard to scream all over the barren valley. The scream echoed off the barren black rocks and no one heard except the depraved followers of Lucre. "No, No," he said. "There can be no kingdom without the children. I must beguile them to come to my kingdom. What can I offer them? I can't have a kingdom without them!" Lucre screamed over and over. Then the thought hit Lucre, "I'll persuade them with the thought of freedom and independence."

Regaining some thought he said, "I have lies and lies is what they'll get! The King may everything else, but He cannot offer lies! I will weave the most desirable lies possible. First they will be lies of beauty but once I have control of their mind, the lies will become destructive if they don't agree to help me. Even if I have nothing real to offer, the lies will seem real if I can convince the children to believe them. That is the power they have and I will use it against them unless they help me. I want what the King has and these silly children are the only way for me to get it." Lucre could only produce what he was so everything he produced was a lie. Everything must produce after its own kind. That was the King's decree. Now the question became, would the children recognize Lucre for what he was?

Lucre withdrew into a dark cave for days and pouted, trying to think up his next move. After some time he emerged with one intent on his mind. He called his gang together. Lucre knew he could not compete with the King's truth when all he had was lies. "My lies will disintegrate when exposed to the light and then I'll be laughed at," was his conclusion after many days of thought. He had to admit that truth ruled even him.

Emerging with his plan formulated he announced, "The mission from this day forward is to steal, kill and destroy anything to do with the children of the King." Informing the renegade followers of his plan, Lucre had decided that if he could not have a Kingdom; he would cause the King's precious children to destroy themselves and others until there was not one left. But first he would have to lure them away from the King. "The children will be lured into these miserable surroundings and forced to stay here just as we are," he hissed.

"How are we to get the children?" his gang wanted to know. The King's protection is upon them." Lucre said, "They will have to come of their own choice, you idiot! You know they have to choose to follow us. If danger cannot come to them, they can come to the danger," he laughed.

"We will have to convince them to come with us, convince them to leave the King. Remember the King has given each of them freedom to choose, if they choose to follow us no one can stop them. Not even the King. Yes he even made a way for those that caused the unknown child to die to be forgiven?"

"That was pretty sneaky bringing that child back to life, but He can't make them follow Him if they choose not to. No he will never leave them, so we have to get them to leave him." Lucre's gang was relieved to know they were not going to have to face the King again; it was best to stay away from him. "Who knew, maybe he would forget them. They sure hoped so."

"No." Lucre said, "Whispering lies and using illusions will convince the children to come. They have everything in the Kingdom they could ever need, but we have one thing we can use thanks to that silly young couple. Doubt has entered into their precious Kingdom and we will use to our advantage. After all there can be trust so long as we cause doubt. Without trust in the King they will be as helpless as lost sheep. A confused sheep will go to the wolf as quickly as he will go to the shepherd. Why my lies are as enticing as the real thing until you test them and by the time that happens it will be too late. All we have to do is convince them to follow our way."

"Why would anyone choose to come here?" ask one of Lucre's gang." "I sure don't want to be here."

"We'll just have to make our lies so desirable they can't resist. Desires are the way to control their actions. You just be sure to whisper those sweet lies very softly and seductively over and over into their ears until they began to imagine what it is we whisper. Pretty soon we'll have a seed planted deep into their hearts and they'll set out to accomplish the desire. Only after we have them will they realize it was all just a lie. Then we'll switch the lies to harsh ugly possibilities and frighten the little darlings out of the silly little minds. " At that Lucre and the entire gang burst into laughter. "Let's give it a try. Whisper something nice and soft to me," Lucre teased.

So Lucre began to sneak to the outer edges of the perimeters surrounding the garden trying to entice the children over to his side. After much time had passed, there were many children who had strayed over believing the lies spoken by Lucre. But once there the lie was exposed.

The children would become ashamed, confused and fear became dominant in their lives due to the constant barrage of lies being spoken by Lucre. The emotion of guilt brought with it a spirit of depression. This spirit was not like the Spirit given by the King. The spirit of depression grew from seeds of darkness and it thrived in the dark dink place they were lured to. The heaviness of the spirit made it hard for the children to speak the teachings of the King. Without speaking the King's words they soon began to forget them. Someone would have to recall the King's words if their mind was to agree and release the Spirit of the King.

It was during the first years when children were foolishly following Lucre that Christian was kidnapped. Christian and his mother along with others worked tirelessly to show the children how it had been in the beginning. Aldolphina was grateful to try and make things right in the garden. Not just for the King but the other children. Now that she was a mother, she felt a strong sense of protection for all children.

In addition to teaching the other children, they were part of a patrol unit formed to protect the outer edges of the garden. Although it would have been safer to stay away from the outer edges, the group fearlessly went to where the danger was to save the other children. It wasn't because of they had special abilities, but because each day they sought wisdom and strength from the King before going out. The group knew their strength was totally dependent on the King and never again would they trust themselves or anyone else to do only what the King could do. Aldolphina having learned this lesson the hard way made sure the others knew the folly of not following the King's way. The group sang songs and encouraged each other as they patrolled the area.

On this day they had been patrolling the outer edges of the garden looking for any children that might be tempted by Lucre's lies. By now everyone was aware of the dangers of going near the outer edges but many of the children did anyway. The patrol unit was there to remind the children of the King's provisions within the Kingdom. Anyone being tempted was told of the King's promises for those who obeyed. Most would come back in near the King.

Evil Pythons also lurked in the shadows to entice the child to venture outside the safety of the garden. The Pythons slithered in and out of the garden to lure the children within Lucre's reach across the boundary.

Both Christian and Aldolphina knowing the power in the King's words had no fear of the Pythons. They had seen the power which had been given them because of the unknown child. They were followers of the unknown child and there were other followers also. The followers patrolled the garden day and night, determine to save innocent children.

Christian and Aldolphina strolled along in no hurry enjoying the company of each other. There was a group of followers further ahead but mother and son stayed together. Later Christian would remember and cherish the last moments they spent together before what happen next. Aldolphina was lost in a story of the early days. Christian loved her stories so much and he was totally absorbed in the story of his mother and father. Aldolphina told of her closeness with the horses and how Cyrill enjoyed creating new things for the King's approval. The Sun was shining and somewhere to the left and behind them, the distant sound of a brook could be heard. All around there was harmony. Earlier they had prevented four children from being lured away by Lucre's magic and there was a warm feeling of victory about the pair.

Then without warning, Lucre and several members of his gang

appeared from among the trees. Lucre recognized the girl from long ago and determined to snatch her. Without realizing it while lost in each other the two had strayed close enough to the edge for Lucre to grab his old friend by the arm. Christian summoned all the power given him by the unknown child and fought Lucre and the others to save his mother.

Hearing the commotion behind them, the other followers turned just in time to see Christian disappear into the tree lined path. Yes Christian had save Aldolphina but Lucre and several of his gang had worked together to snatch Christian. The same power that had brought the unknown child back from death was at work in Christian. Christian felt the power and a spirit of calmness took over his being. Fear could enter his heart and he wondered, "How had Lucre's gang overcome him? Whatever the reason Christian knew His Father's Spirit was in him and soon His Father would come too.

When Christian was brought into the barren valley, some of the captured children recognized him. They thought, "Surely the Father will come now. If he didn't come for us surely he will come for him." When Lucre heard the other children murmuring he knew he had someone special.

Having failed to grab Aldolphina, Lucre did not know he had her child. The unknown child had taught the boy to war in the way of the King since his birth. "What is your name," Lucre asks him. Christian stood up without hesitation and spoke with pride, not one hint of fear in him and said, "I am a child of the King." Lucre was not impressed, because many of the children started out strong but many grew weak with time. Lucre thought, "Perhaps this one knows how to use the King's powers. Maybe I can bribe him." One thing about Lucre he was persistent in his attempts even though he knew he would lose.

Lucre using cunning lies offered the boy half of his kingdom trying to get the boy to reveal if he had power. But the young boy kept repeating, "I listen only to the voice of the King and I will not follow the voice of another." Over and over the boy kept repeating the words of the King, constantly ignoring Lucre and all the things he said.

After several days like this, Lucre became enraged. Although he wanted everyone to be afraid, he knew he had not the power to kill the young boy or any of the children. Therefore it would do no good to threaten him with death. He would have to use the power of suggestion.

Lucre found this ploy to be especially effective when the unsuspecting victim was quiet and their mind unengaged. All the members of the Pythons were recruited to whisper the name of different plagues to the victim while describing the symptoms. Using observation and careful attention to detail Lure cronies would watch to see if the victim favored an itch or rubbed an area of soreness. Then the gang would poke and pinch the victim in that area to convince the victim he or she had symptoms of the plague. This ploy could be used to induce self pity, hopelessness, anger and even hatred.

Right now all forces were at work to convince the boy to accept the plagues suggested to him. With a less informed child the ploy might have worked. It had in times passed. But Christian was well versed in the power he processed through the King and especially now that the unknown child had been sacrificed for his strength and power.

So for many days the forces of evil at Lucre command attempted to break the boy's spirit with suggested plagues and mishaps. They used magic and every tool available to him to make the symptoms appear just as he suggested. A suggestion of hideous lumps would be spoken to the boy while the cronies and magic was used to make lumps appear on his body.

Each time Christian declared, "Because the unknown child's blood has been spilled, no plague can enter my earthly body." Christian knew the sentence for disobedience to the King's law could be plagues and even the sleep of death, but he also knew the King and the unknown child had worked out the compensation. That was why the unknown child was allowed to sleep the death sleep for three days. Then the King sent the power of resurrection to wake him up because the debt was compensated. Never again did a child of the King need suffer any plague or the sleep of death.

Plagues were only allowed to come upon the children if they did not accept the price paid by the unknown child for all disobedience. Because the blood of the unknown child had bled out; the penalty for disobedience was cancelled if the children would accept the unknown child as being the King's own Son. "Was this not the message he and his mother had been telling to save the others?"

"How could Lucre attempt to fool him by constantly trying to break down his love for the King?" Telling him that if the King was so great, why didn't he come for him? He tried many lies to convince the boy the King did not care for him. Every time Lucre sense the boy was weakening and thought he was making progress, somehow the boy would regain strength. "The King had promised never to leave him and he never did."

Christian although young and alone, could feel the King with him even if he couldn't see him. The King is always true to his word and the boy could be heard to say, "I can bear all things through his strength." And strength was what the King gave the boy. After many months and much frustration Lucre had the young boy thrown into the pigpen to tend the pigs and hogs.

After this disgrace, Lucre was more determined than ever to capture the children Even if he couldn't build a Kingdom he wanted to steal what belonged to the King. "If the other children learned the knowledge possessed by this boy, they could defeat him." Lucre and his gang hung around the edge of the Kingdom, (they were forbidden to come in) trying to entice the children to come out of the garden. Lucre found many ways to use the desires of the children against them. That's because the children forgot no other desire should be before the desire to obey the King.

Although the King supplied all the needs of the children, sometimes the children became impatient and didn't wait for the King. It was these times that Lucre found it easy to fool the children. By making the children think they could get their desires on their own, Lucre tricked them into making foolish decisions and often these decisions cause the children to leave the safety of the Kingdom. As soon as they stepped outside the Kingdom boundaries, Lucre was quick to capture them for his use.

Once he had captured them, he no longer pretended to please them, but went right to work making life miserable for them, just as he had done with Christian. Most of the children were not as strong as Christian and they believed the lies Lucre told them. Lucre told them the King would never come because they had disobeyed. The children believed the lie and lost all hope.

As the children lost their hope, they also lost their peace. Christian spent many days encouraging the children to remember the words of the King. "The King will never lie," he repeated over and over to the children. Christian knew that peace was the key to the King's strength and so he constantly declared peace upon the children. "A declaration spoken in conviction would produce the spoken results," the unknown child had said over and over. But the only way for the children to obtain the results was to totally believe the King's words. Lucre made the children believe that because of their mistakes the King had stopped loving them; however that was very much untrue.

Lucre did this by planting thoughts into the children's minds using the method called suggestion. By insinuating untrue events, Lucre caused the children to envision disasters. Now remember the King created the earth with his thoughts so any suggestion that produces thought can control a child of the King. Thoughts will induce spoken words to form giving authority to the spirit to produce the thought. Words spoken by a child of the King are Royal words with authority.

It was in this way the unknown child was also born from the King's thoughts. A helper was sent to speak the words of the child's birth and the King's Spirit planted the baby in a female of pure love after she believed the spoken word. The spoken word then became the unknown child. This child was not made like the other children. This child not only had the King's Spirit, but he was the King's word. The King's word gives authority to the Spirit making this child the authority of all living things since it is the spirit which gives life. Thoughts are powerful.

The King warned the children to think on pure things of the light and to never hide mistakes. Hidden mistakes reside in darkness. Admitting mistakes and seeking forgiveness allowed the children's thoughts to remain in the light. Mistakes brought into the light were wiped away and the children remained clean. Lucre wanted the children in the darkness where his harmful suggestions could take root and grow into destruction upon the children.

Christian, his mother and followers who learned from the unknown child spread this knowledge among the children after the unknown child died. Because he had lived among the children the unknown child could relate to the problems they faced. Guilt was robbing the children of their peace, making it hard for them to believe the King had forgiven them. The garments woven from the blood of the unknown child was upon the children but they found it hard to release their guilt because of Lucre's suggestions.

The King speaks through the heart, but a guilty heart cannot hear the King. Lucre counted on this and instructed his followers to be ready for any stray children. "As soon as a child strays within whispering distance go to work reminding them of past bad deeds and encourage them to come with you where there is no right or wrong," Lucre said. "The thought of having no right or wrong choices appeals to the children's doubt. If there is no right or wrong there can be no King," he laughed.

Although the blood and death of the unknown child made the way for the children's immunity, until each child accepted the payment by testifying for the Kingdom the King was not able to give them another chance. That meant the spirit inside a child who had not testified was still dying.

Realizing how the death of the unknown child had helped the children; Lucre was intent on causing harm to any child that did not have the full knowledge of the unknown child. It was important to catch the children before the spirit was given new life. Lucre set out to entrap any unsuspecting children he could lure over to his hellish hole before they found out the truth of the unknown child.

Now Christian had learned of all these things from the King and knowing what the King's plan was gave him strength to endure the pain when Lucre ordered him to be beaten. Many years passed and Christian was beaten often, but he was not afraid because he knew the King's plan. If Christian had not known the King's plan by knowing his words, Christian would have been afraid like the other children. Christian knew he would get out of this place, but while he was here it was important he teach the other children the King's words so that they too could escape this place and get back to the King.

The children were all living without hope, because they didn't understand the love of the King and the unknown child. After years of living with Lucre beating their minds down with all his lies, the children had forgotten all the King's promises. Some of the children had been here so long they had never heard the King's promises. But Christian knew it was his job to change that.

Christian had to first tell the children the King's promise if they were to believe the promise and not the lies of Lucre. The secret meetings must continue. The message of the unknown child's blood had to get into the children's hearts. The children needed to know that the blood of the King's son was above everything else on this earth and in the heavens, just as the King himself is above everything. That blood had paid the price for all their mistakes.

Once he could get them to believe then they could speak directly to the King. Everyone had to speak to the King for himself. The only way the King could save them was if they ask to be saved. They would have to speak to the King.

During this time Christian sometimes became so tired that he almost forgot all of the teachings about the King; but he struggled until the words came back. Sometimes he had conversations with the King just as though he was there and the words came back. It was the conversation of prayer. Christian knew that the King heard him and brought the words back to his remembrance. These words had the power to bring him and the others back home.

It was important to bring as many children as possible back home. Hearing the truth would give them opportunity to accept the blood garments made available by the unknown child. Once they believed, they could speak to the King and He would grant them immunity for all past crimes against the Kingdom. They would be free to go home.

But before anyone left for home, he must rescue Gayla.

CHAPTER SEVEN

Preparing for Battle

Christian struggled to get up out of the mud. It was hard, this struggle. The mud caked his face, arms hands and everywhere. But worst of all the mud got into ears and eyes, clouding his vision and preventing him from hearing clearly. This anomaly of life effected aspect of his being. It had been so long since he last felt clean. How he longed for the peace of his Father's Kingdom. That life was so long ago.

Pushing himself up with both hands strength surged through his body. "I will not be defeated. I am a child of the King and all power belongs to me!" he shouted.

No matter how long it took, Christian vowed that with the help of his Father he would get back home and so he declared with his mouth the truth of the Father's word. "There is no room for failure. I have been given power over all works of evil." Speaking the words out loud gave encouragement in an ambiguous situation. The situation may be hazy, but because the words were his Father's words, the outcome was guaranteed, his Father could not lie. This was his confidence as he strode forth determined to win. The words gave life to his desire and he could actually feel his victory.

But just getting himself back would not be enough; Christian knew he had to get the others back also. Maybe not everyone, but the Kingdom was open to all who would believe and he knew there were believers among the children.

Christian thought back to the day he struggled with Lucre for Aldolphina. The strength that had sailed through his body had not been his own, but that of the King's. It was this type of strength he was feeling now. This same strength would sustain the children once they had enough faith to ask for it, and then they would realize it was available at all times. Yes there were times he felt weak, but inside he knew that strength would come if he should ever need it.

The Father's strength came only when his strength was at its' lowest. In this way his strength increased just as though he had an armor bearer. The armor bearer was at hand any time his scabbard became empty so that he was never without ammunition to fight with. The King was his armor bearer, always ready with a fresh sword.

So it is in this fight of faith, the King would not let him carry more than he had muscle to carry, but He would always see that he had adequate weapons. Conviction in his believeth of the King's promises assured him of a ready supply of strength. If at any point his weapons became low, reliance on the King's word would renew his strength. Nothing could withstand the arsenal of words which were the King's promises to His children.

Just as the King promised, he would never leave him or any of his children. However he wanted his children to grow in their own strength. He had created the earth with words; the children could rule the earth with words if they remain loyal to him. The choice was theirs, either blessings or curses, but His principles were firm

In the days since the abduction of Gayla, Christian had been doing just that; building his strength through training. He constantly reminded himself, "If I speak and act in believeth of the King, I will be empowered to succeed. If I allow doubt in my identity as to who I am as the King's son and the power of the King, I will bring the curse of failure upon myself and possible those with me." The young boy set his face like flint. The boy's body was taunt with conviction of his victory because of who he was.

Remembering the King's promises gave strength to his mind and speaking the King's promises gave strength to his heart. It was time to show his believeth by taking action.

Reaching the encampment and brushing the dirt from his eyes, he realized there was an excitement in the air. Going in search of Chen, Christian continued to reinforce his thoughts with purpose while thinking "I won't give up and I won't lose. I will soar like an eagle." Using caution to approach Chen he slowed his walk while preparing for an argument to convince the ridiculer into fighting with him to secure Gayla's release.

"Even if Chen did not believe in the King, there was no doubting his love and respect for the girl. Surely he would help save the girl," Christian reason to himself. Rounding the corner, Christian was unprepared for the sight ahead of him. There with Chen was a large crowd. At first glance his heart quickens. "Has something happen to Gayla?" he asks himself. Then to his surprise, he realized everyone was laughing. Joy was a rare thing here, but here was everyone cheering. Christian didn't know what to make of it.

Touching the nearest person while trying to appear casual Christian asks, "What is the great news?" The boy whom Christian touched turned with a big smile and said, "Haven't you heard?" "Where have you been, asleep? For four days we won't have to work and there is to be a BIG Party, starting tonight!" The boy moved off in excitement to celebrate with the other cheering people. The people were so excited they had temporarily forgotten where they were. Once again they were being blinded by Lucre's tricks.

Christian knew the battle had just gotten harder. "Now why would Lucre do such a thing," Christian wondered aloud? At that moment a large wooden wagon pulled up, drawn by two huge black horses snorting fire from their nostrils. Their hoofs of the animals were as big as wagon wheels. Anything in their path without speed was in danger of being crushed.

Lucre's thugs settled in the back of the wagon began snarling and growling while throwing items to the excited children. Pantaloons, gowns, dresses, shirts, the likes of which the children had never seen before came flying from the wagon. Shoes! Shoes were a luxury unobtainable for the children. But here they were sailing out into the crowd. "Shoes!" the people screamed. Almost everyone here had never owned a pair of shoes and now they were being bombarded with beautiful leather sandals fit for a King. "Oh no," Christian thought, "This could only mean trouble."

The people were overjoyed. There were wagons with cakes and figs and fruits, there had never been fruits in this place! Never! There were hand carved toys and gadgets to play with. "What!" One girl screamed. "To play with! Surely you jest," she told the goon handing her the toy. The girl was so moved she began to cry. She was thirteen and never had she been able to play as a child.

There were combs and pretty baubles for the older girls. All the people began to dance in circles. "Where had the goods come from?" They were giddy with joy. Everyone ran to prepare for the party.

"But wait, where would they find water? How could they put on the finest clothes they had ever owned when there was thick muddy dirt on their bodies?" several of the older girls wanted to know. Then just like gallant knights, goons driving wagons with big barrels of water pulled up. Now the children were never allowed to wash so this alone was a treat. Even the everyday drinking water contained dirt. Christian knew Lucre was no gallant knight, he wasn't a knight at all; he was a hooligan out to steal, kill and destroy all that he came across.

Someone was holding a pair of black shiny new shoes with gold buckles out to Christian. "Try them and see if they fit. Maybe if you wash some of that mud off your feet, they'll fit," laughed the jubilant youngster. The boy ran away giddy with joy leaving the shoes behind. Christian surveyed the scene with his heart breaking and marveled at how easy it was to please trampled, broken people. These were the beloved children the King loved. The unknown child had died to give freedom to these children. They were more precious than gold and yet they did not know it.

Where there had been no joy at all, now it was if a few pair of shiny shoes could erase all the wicked acts levied upon these people. People who were meant to rule the earth. The King could give so much more and the gifts of the King would never fade or wear out. He had to make his brothers and sisters understand.

Moving deeper into the crowd, Christian finally came up on Chen in the crowd. Excited he ran up to the boy, "Chen I have a plan to get Gayla. We can use the excitement and gaiety of the moment to our advantage." For a moment the smile left Chen's face but just as quickly the smile was back. Speaking in terseness Chen said, "Ah, Christian can't you let up for awhile? First it was the King, now it's Gayla. Don't spoil the fun. Aren't you the one who told us to have joy in our lives? Didn't you say the King would take of care us? Can't I have fun and let your King take care of Gayla's problems?"

Shock filtered slowly down from Christian's face to his entire body forcing him to become weak. The Chen standing before Christian was a stranger. "What has happen to this boy?" Christian wondered to himself. Sure he never believed in the King, but he had never been indifferent to needs of the other children. Using caution, Christian spoke his next sentence slow and deliberate because he was not sure of the boy before him. "Chen this fight is not yours; it's the King's fight. The only thing the King requires of us is that we stand firm on his word and don't ever give in to Lucre tricks and lies. Is that too much to ask if it will free Gayla?"

"Don't be fooled by things that wear out and rust. This moment will pass, but the gifts of the Kings are forever and will never wear out. Lucre is a liar and everything about him is a lie, there is no truth to him. Not even the shiny shoes offered in exchange for your soul are truth and believe me; he will require your soul. Don't you understand the battle is between the King and Lucre? We are only trophies for Lucre, whereas we are children to be loved by the King." Finished speaking, Christian studied the boy before him.

"Christian I know everything can change tomorrow and we'll be back in the mud again, but that's why I want to enjoy today! Boy we had better enjoy today, because we don't know what tomorrow will bring. We are at the mercy of chance and we don't control anything about this life."

Struggling to reach the boy, Christian keep his face calm while making one more attempt, "Chen haven't you heard a word I said to you. With the King every day is to be enjoyed, not just a few days. The King is the same today, tomorrow and everyday. He loves you as much today as he did on the day the unknown child died. Can't you believe the story I told you of the unknown child. I was there. I know it's true. It was love that moved him to a sacrificial death to fulfill the King's law. No one took his life, he gave it for our freedom and he hasn't changed his mind or his love. He fulfilled the requirement of the law and returned to the King so that you don't have to fear Lucre or anyone! All you have to do is believe it was all done out of love for you. Stand firm and allow the King to help us. All you have to do is believe in His love. He will deliver Gayla, Chen. He doesn't love any of us more than the other. He loves all! Trust him Chen."

Without realizing it, Christian allowed his emotions to overpower him. Now pulling himself back together he thought on the word of the King. "Let not your heart be anxious, because I know what you have need of." Bringing the words to recollection allowed Christian to regain his composure.

Looking at Christian as though he were stupid Chen shook his head and stomped off. Christian understood why Chen and the others wanted to relish in the enjoyment of today's events but it was a fallacy to believe any good would come from these devious tricks. Just as Chen had said, they had only known one day at time. They didn't understand or believe the King "had a future of prosperity for them body and soul." The future the King planned for them held good and not evil. No one had ever shown them good, why would they now? The King's plan was for all eternity, not just one day. He had to get the seed of the King's word into their minds, he determined in his heart.

If he could get the word inside the children's mind, the power of the word would bring conviction and then the children could discern right from wrong. With discernment of evil they could ask the King to change their hearts. Christian walked the way Chen had gone muttering to himself, "The power of the word though silent will be revealed and with revelation power will come. The power will free the children."

Continuing through the crowd, Christian was lost in his thoughts. "It wasn't entirely the children's fault they didn't get the word inside their minds as soon as it was spoken. The darkness in their minds was getting thicker each day the light of truth was denied access. The propensity of the earth body was to except words spoken repeatedly, especially when circumstance supported the words. However the more truth they hear; light will penetrate the darkness dominating their minds. Then they will be aware of Lucre's lies." By continuing to speak truth to him, Christian was using truth to strengthen his own resolve.

That's how Lucre stimulated believeth in his lies by repetition and that's how believeth in the King's word was inspired. Of course this was just one more thing Lucre had copied by studying the penchant of the children. But Christian knew there was one major difference; "Truth produces peace and although not understood by the earthly mind, this peace produced strength to overcome all adversity. Peace will ensure victory! First peace comes, then victory. I know truth will win out, but first the children must hear the truth. Trust comes by hearing the truth over and over again until it produces the inner peace which will make available their full confidence in the power behind the truth of the King's word. Then and only then will the light be able to dispel the darkness in their minds and hearts."

Suddenly in the middle of his pep talk, all thought was lost. It was as though Christian's mind hit a huge boulder. Right before him was Chen talking to the 'Clean up' gang. The Clean up gang was the name given to a group of children who had sworn alliance to Lucre and his goons. They were called the Clean up gang because they were called in to clean up what was left of the elders let into the dog pens.

Both girls and boys were in the gang. These children had lost hope and were now as depraved as Lucre and his goons. Christian had no fear of the children, but that was just the problem. They were children and not evil goons. Even these children deserved to be freed of this horrible place but power in the wrong hands could cause hurt for a lot of people. "Was Chen sharing the King's word from the meetings with this group? Oh no," Christian groaned. "Was that how Lucre got on to Gayla? One more problem and still he had to find her. Whatever Lucre was planning with all the festivities was not in their best interest."

Christian stumbled away from the crowd and peering around started toward the main house. "Maybe he could catch a glimpse of Gayla." Not only did he need to save her but he really needed to see another believer right now. With everyone's attention on the festivities, it wasn't hard for Christian to get close to the house.

Walking around the edge of the yard, he dropped down on his belly as he got closer. Worming his body through the ashen mud, Christian caught sight of the young girl setting on a large bed of black stones. "Could that be Gayla?" The girl's shoulders were slumped and she appeared to be much older than Gayla. Looking closer Christian thought it was an elder. Then she raised her head and he saw that it was Gayla.

It did not appear to be the Gayla he knew. The Gayla he knew had a brilliant smile. This girl was like a ghost of that Gayla. "What had they done to her?" But even as he ask himself the question, he could see enormous amounts of abuse had been inflicted upon the girl. No doubt Lucre's men were the guilty parties. Anger clouded his judgment and he instinctively ran out into the open toward the hurting figure.

Just then three grotesque creatures came around the corner of the house leading a large black dog. The dog was the size of a small horse. The dog's nostrils immediately seized upon the boy's smell. Teeth bared and nostrils flaring the dog strained toward Christian. Not until that very moment did Christian spot a huge rock. It was as though it appeared out of nowhere. Quickly he jumped on top of the rock banishing a stick he picked up as he leapt up. "Where had the rock come?" He didn't recall seeing it as he made his mad dash toward Gayla.

The stick in his hand was of no size needed to beat back such a large animal. Christian would not let fear of the animal or its' holder take hold of him. Using the anger to had conviction to his words he chanted, "No weapon formed against me shall succeed. I am a child of the only King!"

Suddenly to the amazement of all three, the huge animal tucked his tail between his legs and began to whimper trying to run back the other way. Caught off guard the goon holding the animal let him go. Looking first at the animal then at Christian the malefactor shook his fist at Christian saying, "Don't move! I'll be back for you!" and took off after the dog.

Rejoicing Christian threw his arms up and let out a loud yell of thanks to his unseen King. Christian knew the King had saved him.

A different goon with hair covering his arms and legs wearing a belt made of chains and keys around his waist entered the yard. He had been instructed to come for a boy seen in the yard. The keys were so loud you could the clanking sound even from where Christian had run to the other side of the yard, but they had help to mask Christian's yell. Christian had heard about those keys.

Deep down inside the house there were dark little holes covered by grates more than two feet thick. The keys fit the locks on these grates, but once you were locked in one of those holes, you were never seen again. Everyone in the compound called them one-way keys.

Christian backed out of sight behind a large black mound. Everything here was covered in black ashes from the burning mountains. Christian lay still looking in Gayla's direction. The goon was searching for his charge. Christian held his breath, afraid to move. Christian squeezed his eyes shut in case the villain could see the white of his eyes. Then for no apparent reason, the odious goon stopped and walked back toward the girl on the mound.

Just as Christian looked again in that direction, Gayla with the slightest action raised her hand as if to brush away her hair. Christian knew in his gut that she had seen him and was signaling for him to go, but now there was light in the eyes that had been dull.

Christian felt a sickness in his stomach; it was too hard to see her like that. He was enervated and felt as though he would throw up. Crawling on his belly, he got far enough away to stand. Christian started to run as fast as he could, trying to forget the image of the beautiful girl who now looked like an old woman. By the time he reached the pigpen his chest hurt from the running. For the first time ever the dirty stinky pigpen felt like shelter from the rest of the camp.

Never had he held so tightly to this filthy pigpen. At this moment he felt security here. It was the safest place in this valley of doom. The worst feeling of being alone came over Christian. He was so totally alone without anyone in the world. He felt hopeless.

Just this morning he had risen with determination in his heart, ready to fight. Now just a short time later events were causing him to feel hopeless. "What am I to do!" he yelled at the fat ugly hog. Shaking his fist in the air, Christian called for his King but only silence answered him.

It had been easier to remain determined until he saw her like that. But wait, there was the problem. "I'm letting my eyes believe rather my heart! Of course didn't the King say, "I would overcome by confessing the blood sacrifice of His son?" I can't believe with my eyes, I must believe his provision for overcoming obstacles." Feelings of relief flooded his being because he recognized how close he had come to giving in to the lie of Lucre. Christian stepped into a feeling of restful peace. The image of Gayla had overshadowed the image of his father temporarily but now he was alert.

That's what Lucre desired, for the appearance of circumstance to overcome the truth of the King. "The truth of the matter is the King is all powerful and with him on my side, "No weapon can ever defeat me."" The image of a battle from long ago entered his mind. He had been patrolling when a ravenous lion had run amok among the children. Christian having just finished listening to the unknown child ran toward the lion speaking words of victory. Christian hit the lion with a rock that did not appear large enough to inflict serious injury upon the lion but in an instant the lion lay dead.

It was then that Christian understood all the unknown child had taught him about words having power. Christian knew it was not the rock that had slay the lion, but the determination his words planted in his heart had produce faith in the outcome of that battle. That was because the words spoke of the King's desire for his child to have dominion and when he spoke those words, he was in agreement with the King. It was the law of the King that when his children walked in agreement with him, they would have success.

"The principles and laws had not changed. Today it was the King's desire for his children to succeed and he would speak and walk in agreement with the wishes of the King. Any who would believe in the King, could be more than the King's creation, they would be called sons and daughters of the King. They would become Royalty with every right to rule," Christian spoke all these things to encourage himself in this fight.

There was great relief in having avoided the pit Lucre had set for him. "Whew, I almost give in to pity and hopelessness. I must remember that just as the unknown child said, "The war has been won; this is only one more battle in a string of victories with a definite outcome." The outcome is victory. Why should I fear or tremble?"

Christian wasn't sure when it happen but at sometime while he spoke, he was no longer hopeless and deep inside he felt as though he had been rescued from destruction. He knew everything was all right. Strength rose up in him. Thoughts were building up his confidence. No matter what it looked like right now, he knew it would get better and better until they were all home.

The presence of his Father could be felt in the hog pen. Oh how good that calming strong presence felt to the young boy. Peace came over Christian and although the problems with Gayla had not changed, Christian was no longer anxious about it. He knew everything would be alright.

Experiencing a calming peace, Christian lay down and slept. He surrendered all thought and worry to the King. While the boy slept, the helper Maylene appeared in a dream. Standing behind Maylene in battle formation were hundreds of helpers. Arrayed in golden battle helmets and carrying swords of red hot metal they sang, "Hail to the King, our Lord."

Maylene carried a pail and bent to wash the mud from the young boy. As she dipped her cloth into the pail it could be seen that the pail was filled with blood. Dipping the cloth, Maylene began to clean first his face, working her way down his naked body. Just as she finished cleaning the boy, the unknown child appeared before him as though standing in mid air. The pail of blood had become a golden goblet. It too was filled with blood.

Maylene handed the golden cup to the unknown child in His right hand. In His left hand was a sword burning hot with heat. Across the sword the letters A-L-L P-O-W-E-R could be read. Christian stood before the unknown child, clothe only in a tunic but clean after being thoroughly washed. The unknown child lifted the golden cup in his right hand and said, "Drink." As Christian open his mouth and began to drank from the cup of blood, what had been hot became cool as it slide smoothly down his throat. The taste was sweeter than honey.

When the last drop had been swallowed, the unknown child took the cup and handed the cup back to Maylene. Horace a second helper stepped forward and handed the most beautiful battle breast plate ever seen to the unknown child. The breast plate was of pure gold inlaid with every precious stone known to man and shone brighter than the sun. Attached was a golden belt to protect his lions. The unknown child burned the breast plate called righteousness into the boy's chest using the white hot sword to secure it and placed the golden belt with the word T-R-U-T-H engraved by heat over the boy's lions. After which He placed the sword in Christian's hand and the hot metal melted to become one with the boy.

Then Maylene stepped forward with a helmet made of one hard shiny diamond and trimmed with every jewel known to man. The helmet sparkled with iridescent magnificence. In the other hand Maylene carried sandals made of three strung cord. Maylene handed both items to the unknown child.

First He placed the helmet on Christian's head and then He kneeled to the ground and securely tied the sandals called peace, one at a time to the boy's feet. Then he stood and looking at Christian He spoke, "You have been given the only battle suit you will ever need except for one item. Everything you have on is my gift. You did nothing to earn them. You could not pay the required price for them. So I paid the price that was required by the King's law because only His love could overcome His law. Do you understand? I ask only that you love as I have loved." Christian acknowledged by nodding yes, but he knew he should not speak.

"Now for the last thing you need for battle." The unknown took a small seed from His mouth, placing the seed in Christian's mouth, he ordered Christian to swallow the seed. As soon as Christian complied with the order, a beautiful bronze battle shield appeared in his hand. The unknown child speaking to Christian said, "The size of the shield is dependent on you. This one thing you control. The shield will grow in proportion to how much food you give it. The food required for the seed to grow is the King's word. The shield will grow to the needed size in each battle you fight if you have feed it with sufficient food. Yes there are many battles ahead for you, but remember I am with you even to the ends of the earth."

Then Christian awoke and there was no one in the pig pen with him, but he was standing on his feet and all traces of mud were gone from his body. Then looking down, Christian saw something glitter in the mud. Bending over he picked up a small golden arrowhead with the figure of a lion stamped on it.

Christian looked around the stark dark hog pen for the last time; he knew he would never be back. Turning Christian headed out the door to complete the purpose he was sent here for.

Christian felt strong and determined to complete the task given him by the King. He felt love for the other children and angry that they were being tricked. The King would handle that Lucre for sure. Christian felt strong and determined to help the others. Yes he would go to the party, but he would not wear any of the clothes provided by Lucre. The only suit he wanted was the suit of armor the unknown child had given him.

Christian stepped out the pigpen and looked around the grounds. The people were excited and running from place to place trying to prepare for the big party. The lighting was dim. The only light came from campfires and the light from the burning mountaintops. The fires within the mountain burned of bright red and yellow. They never went out. The fires made the place very hot and there was not one cool spot.

The fires cast long shadows over the camp floor. With all the people running around the shadows were eerie and appeared to be dancing. In the dim light it was hard to tell which the people were and which were only shadows. The shadows look like dancing devils. Christian set out to find out what Lucre was up to. With his Father's promises behind him, Christian hurried into the frenzied party atmosphere. There was no need to run away from the giant shadows.

Christian stood around the grounds carefully peering into the shadowy faces. The light was very dim now. The answer was here and he was sure he had enough light inside his heart to find it. As Christian walked he saw how Lucre had used meaningless material items such as clothes and trinkets to woo the children. All these things were subject to wear out and rust, but for now they promised a good time as compensation for the miserable life of the children. All this was just another set of tricks to make the children believe that he, Lucre could provide for them. Of course it was a lie. But at this moment even Christian was amazed at how much the lie had lifted the mood for the children. Growing angrier by the moment, Christian wondered how long it would take the children to see how Lucre was tricking them.

What would they be able to do when they realized it? They could do absolutely nothing of their own power. The only way they had of fighting back and winning was to follow the King. Desperately Christian searched the crowd for someone to believe him. Just one believer could help to alter the disaster the children were headed for.

While all these things were happening in Katerboro, many helpers in the Kingdom were busy weaving garments made of the blood of the unknown child. Unbeknown to Christian victory for he and all believers had been assured and preparation was in place with nothing left to chance. Once the children believed, the King would make sure of their success. It was with great satisfaction that the King watched as Christian sought out believers. Believing could only come by hearing and the King knew Christian would speak out.

Christian doing what he felt in his heart scrutinized the grounds for someone to believe, he was sure Lucre was up to no good. Lucre used the children's longing against them. "Everyone longed for happiness, but happiness was dependent on circumstances as much as anguish is. The King wanted to give His children joy. Joy is a state of being, not an emotion. Joy trusts the King to be a good Lord over His children and to provide all things needed for a good life. Why couldn't he get that message through to the children? Contentment even in these circumstances was possible, if they would trust the King's way of escape." This train of thought continued as Christian moved among the crowd. "If no one else believes, I will always wait on the King. He will do all that He has promised."

The King had often cautioned his children about desire. He had explained that in the beginning he had created two desires within them and every other desire came from the two. The first desire the King had given them was the desire for him. The King created the children to be one with him. Without him, they would always feel incomplete.

The second desire he had given his children was the desire for each other. Again the King is love and he knew the need to share love. The King knew the need would keep them from ever being alone. Lucre used the need to love and to be loved to pervert the children's heart with false suggestions more than any other tool. The King had never intended any of his children to be alone. Therefore the need for love was in every child. And for a time the children stayed together through love, until Lucre found a way to use desire and love to destroy the children.

After that the King had warned the children to be careful of the things they let into their hearts. No matter how desperate things seem to be, the heart had to be guarded at all times. The King knew how strong desires of the heart could be and also knew they could be foolish.

Now here Lucre was using the children's desire to get what he wanted. Just like all down trodden people, the children needed something good to happen for them. Lucre was pretending to provide just that. But Christian was not going to give in so easily.

Christian wandered around the site looking for clues as to why Lucre was pretending to care. The deceit must be exposed to the light. Lucre's lies would never stand up to the truth of the King's word once exposed. Down at the south end of the site, Lucre had ordered a huge pit to be built and inside was a bright fire. Over the top of the pit was there was a long rod held up by two tree stumps on either end. The rod was shoved into one end of a large pig and came out of the other end. The pig was being turned slowly over the fire. This had never been done for the children; only Lucre received fresh cooked meat. Tonight there was to be meat for everyone. Lucre was going to great lengths to please his captives. Christian had to find out why.

Christian moved close to the goons turning the hog. The hog was so large there were two of them doing the job. Normally one of the captive children did this job for Lucre. Christian could hear the words spoken by the goons as he crouched in the shadows. "Did you sprinkle the powder on the pig?" "Yes, I can't wait until they start hallucinating. It should make them lose all control in their actions." At that moment, the one nearest Christian turned quickly looking in Christian's direction, "What was that? Who's there?"

Christian had stepped on a twig. Laying very still Christian spoke silently to the King, "Please Father hide me from the evil one." After what seemed a long time, although it was only a couple of seconds, the two men began to laugh with each other. Then one said to the other, "You've been getting that powder in your nose and mouth. You're imagining things; better not let Lucre find out." Christian lay still and he was not afraid, his heart was strong and stout, fixed on the King. "Be still and know that I am here," he could hear the words of the King.

Feeling encouraged by hearing part of the plan, Christian knew he was on to something, still he didn't know what. Lucre was planning to incapacitate the children at least partially. The powder was to alter the state of mind of the children. "Why would he want that? The children were already thinking defeat," Christian thought puzzled.

Starting back to the main party site, Christian was very much aware of the eerie shadows dancing all around. The place was always gloomy, but tonight there was such a ghastly feeling in the air. It was almost as though there were unseen ghost all over.

Upon re-entering the main site Christian spotted several of the older boys. Samuel, Eric and several of the bigger boys were wild with excitement. They were chasing the girls around the large fire. With new clothes and the newly granted freedom, the children had given themselves over to the moment. There was no thought of tomorrow. No one gave thought to why Lucre was acting different. Tonight the entire camp appeared to be lawless. Nothing good could come from this night. "What appears to be freedom would surely be the beginning of the end for the lost children, were it not for the King, thought Christian.

Several of the elders were drinking from strange bottles. Most days there was barely water to quench the thirst of this hot dry place, but tonight there was no end to the strange bottles that were being passed around. The party was going at a heady speed.

Christian wondered about Gayla, was she O K? She was no longer at the site where he saw her earlier. He checked after leaving the pig pen. The party was for everyone, but Gayla was not here. "Had she been locked away somewhere?" Christian had so many concerns and there were so many needs to take care of. Where was Gayla? What was Lucre up to? Christian was beginning to feel overcome. Looking around Christian sought a quiet place. A short distance away was a jutted crag. Christian decided to set there. "From there I'll have a clear view of the campsite," he thought.

Before he could set down on the cliff, Christian heard a muffled sound from nearby. Hunching down close to the earth he quietly stole over to the side from which the sound came from. The shock of what he saw almost made Christian cry out. Bound and gagged, hands tied above her head to a pole was Gayla. Christian started toward the girl and stopped, before moving into a position that might harm himself as well as Gayla; he made a silent petition to the King for protection.

He knew he could not save her on his own, but the King could. Finishing the request to the King, he did not hesitate and moved with confidence to the bound girl. He had made his petition known and the King would answer. Christian removed the gag from her mouth first. "I'll get water," Christian said. "No," Gala said in an urgent whisper. The girl was so weak; she barely had strength to speak. It was obvious she had been beaten, probably to tell where he was. If only she had more training in the word of the King to avoid the blows from these goons. "There's no time! Lucre is looking for you. He intends to burn both you and me tonight after the crowd is drunk with his evil spell.

Christian was not fearful at the words spoken. Christian's heart was fixed on the word of his Father. He would not be swayed by bad news and besides Lucre had no power to harm him or Gayla. "Yes Gayla there is time. Hold on, you must have water. I'll get it and return." Christian loosely placed the gag over Gala's mouth in case anyone should look in on her. Running as fast as his legs would carry him back to the pigpen, skirting around the party, his mind raced ahead of his feet. He needed to get water for Gayla but he could not trust the water the party. "There is a small vessel with water in the pig pen. Looks like I'll have to make one more trip there," he thought.

Now he knew Lucre's plan was to stop him from talking. Lucre had no power to kill him because knowing how to use the authority of the King's word gave him authority over Lucre's tricks. "So," he wondered, "how does Lucre intend to accomplish this? It doesn't matter, I am not afraid," he thought. "The King is always prepared to step into any situation involving his children. So long as I do not allow fear to block my spiritual gateway and continue to speak the King's words, I will not be defeated." Christian felt the King's strength surging through his body.

Christian had reached the pigpen and grabbed the small vessel of water. Rounding the pigpen, he ran smack into Chen and spilled most of the water. "Chen in a drunken haze said, "You don't need water Chris, Lucre has given us special drinks for tonight. It's much better than anything we had before. Here have some. I have an extra bottle."

Christian looked at the vessel in his hand and at the water on the ground already soaking into the black mud. Chen stood before him, eyes half closed with a silly grin on his face. "I spoke to the Clean-up crew today. They're all prepared to take you in if you stop this silly talk about a King. Did I tell you, I joined their group? Well I will be in once I complete my initiation. They'll let me know what I need to do." Chen was more locked into Lucre's darkness than ever before and Christian felt fear for the young boy.

He could not become angry over the spilled water. Anger would block his communication with the King. No, the King's law prohibited communication with His children when they were angry with one another. This law had been established to ensure the children treated each other with love.

Because of the King's goodness, he could have no part of anything or anyone bad. In the same way He would never reward bad behavior or thoughts, so all communication was blocked until the anger was taken care of. As much as the King loved his beloved children, if they allowed evil into their hearts it would prevent the King from touching them directly and Christian knew that anger was very bad.

If he allowed anger to take hold of him, the most the King would be able to do would be to build a hedge of protection around him until he got rid of the anger. That would be precious time wasted because he needed the King to move on his behalf to prevent the evil Lucre had planned for this night.

There would be no point in trying to reason with Chen in his present condition. So Christian smiled at the drunken boy, "You know what I'll do, I'll hold this while you go and get more," Christian said while taking the bottle from Chen. "Now run and be quick."

Chen began a drunken slur, "Christian you've got to loosen up and forget all this talk about a King. Look, I'm really sorry about that friend of yours that got killed. What did you call him, an unknown child? Poor guy had bad luck to get killed like that without anyone knowing who he was. But you've got to let all this talk about His blood saving the children go. Lucre has said that after tonight things will be better here for all of us." "Yes I know Lucre intends for things to be different. Now hurry and get those bottles," Christian said while pasting a big grin on his face.

As Chen staggered away mumbling to himself, the tears welled up in Christian's eyes. It hurt so much to see Chen under Lucre's spell when he knew the beautiful life his Father had intended for Chen to have. Lucre was stealing something very precious from all of them, but many times the King had said, "When a thief is caught, he must pay back seven times that which he stole." "I sure hope the children receive seven times the joy taken from their lives," Christian said out loud.

Christian looked into the vessel and saw only a small amount of water was left inside. Looking up, Christian lifted his head toward the sky and whispered, "Father where shall I get water?" The water in the vessel had been all that remained of his ration for several days to come and he could not risk the party area now that he knew Lucre's intentions.

At that moment it was as though he heard the King speak, "The water I give, she shall thirst no more." Looking into the vessel, Christian saw that it was filled to the top with water. Joy filled Christian's heart just as the water had filled the vessel. Christian knew he was not alone. He wasted no time in getting back to Gayla.

CHAPTER EIGHT

The Mountains Erupt

Setting alone in the dark waiting for Christian's return, Gayla began to recite some of the words Christian had taught her during the times in the pigpen. "Although I walk through the valley of the shadow of death, I shall not fear for his rod and his staff shall comfort me." Christian had said this referred to a good shepherd who guided his sheep with a stick and a walking cane. The good shepherd also use the stick and cane to protect his sheep from wild animals. The unknown child was like a good shepherd.

Gayla found comfort in the words as she imagined a King with a rod of power and a staff of goodness. In her mind Gayla could see the King dressed like a shepherd chasing all bad animals away. The thought made the girl smile. Gayla felt certain that Christian's King would save her and her heart felt peace.

Remembering the day the evil fiends came after her brought back the feeling of fear. Once more she wanted to scream for help, but there was no one to hear her. There was no one to help. It was during this time of knowing she was alone, she came to realize that she had nothing but the words of a boy who believed in a very powerful King to give her hope. If he was not real then she was lost.

Gayla surrendered every hope she had to this King. If he was there it was up to him to save her. Then suddenly she felt she was not alone. Although she had never met this King, she knew for certain he was real. For the first time, the King made His presence felt by her. It was as though she could reach out and touch him and the feeling left her wanting more. The truth of the words spoken by Christian rang out within her heart and it felt good.

The words gave Gayla comfort and, she was no longer afraid. The guards watching the girl noticed a difference in her attitude from the way she sat. No longer was her back bent with her face toward the ground. The guards weren't sure when the change took place but now the girl was setting erect with head up and was that a smile on her face? The girl appeared to be at peace.

Seeing that Gayla was not afraid, they began to taunt her, calling her dumb and daft trying to evoke fear from her. But remembering the mysterious feeling of her King's presence gave her the confidence to look straight into the faces of her tormentors and to declare that "the King was coming to save her." For on that day she accepted Him as her King.

This of course made the men laugh. But still they moved farther away from her after tighten the chains as tight as possible around her waist. The ones holding her arms let go and backed away. There was something different about the girl and they were a little leery.

When they had reached the big house on the dreadful day they came for her; she had been dragged before Lucre. One of the fiends spoke in low tones to Lucre. Afterwards Lucre summoned for Gayla to be brought before him. He questioned her over and over. Gayla had told Lucre of Christian's King and how he created everything in the world. Lucre had bristled with rage. Yelling, "That idiot boy has been spreading information about the King right under my very nose. I have been tricked!"

But suddenly the anger faded and Lucre started to look panicky. "What if the King is on his way at this very moment?" Lucre told the guards, "Chain the foolish girl outside" and he went into hiding waiting to see if the King would come. When the King didn't come that day Lucre devised a way to be rid of the girl and that silly boy. "Maybe the boy is an idiot like the other children and doesn't really know how to contact the King," he mused.

"Take the girl out and chain her within sight. Don't touch her just yet but make sure she has a guard at all times," he ordered. He was sure she would draw Christian sooner or later and when she did, he would be ready. Lucre cooked up the plans for a big celebration. "Here is my chance to really get service from those idiot children. The idiots missed up the plan I laid for that unknown child, but this time there is no King around. He doesn't come into Katerboro so there will be no interference when I get rid of these two. There will be plenty of intoxicating drink for the children.

The celebration will not only draw that meddlesome Christian out, but combine with the poisonous liquor; it will be the means to get rid of both the boy and the girl. Once the children get their fill, I'm sure that Clean up gang will be willing to carry out my plan." That was the place where Christian found Gala chained that day.

Christian stood before Gayla now offering the water. The thirsty girl took several long, deep drinks before stopping. Feeling refreshed Gayla said, "Christian call your Father! I don't know the whole plan but Lucre means to destroy you. Your Father can come with his army and save you."

"Gayla you mustn't be afraid. I have petition the King this very night. Even now Gayla he is with you and me. He is forever present even if you don't see him, believe me He is here. Do you believe me?" Gayla was so excited. "Oh yes Christian. I too have experienced the King's presence! I believe you when you say He's here." Strength and calmness gave her peace and she knew that the words Christian spoke were true. The gaunt haggard look was gone from her appearance. Instead there was a joyful look of anticipation. She didn't understand how, but she knew the King was right here with them, she could feel him. He felt like love.

Taking a closer look into Gayla's eyes, Christian's confidence was renewed. Yes Gayla was changed. Bending over Christian hugged the girl with joy. Suddenly Gayla felt her whole body fill with joy. This joy she had never felt before, but she knew it would give her strength.

"Christian, not only does Lucre intend to destroy you, but he wants to find all the believers here and destroy them as well. Lucre said, "His only job is to destroy all believers wherever he finds them. He said he has to pay back the King for kicking him out. Christian did Lucre live with the King at one time?"

"Yes Gayla, at one time he did, but he was disobedient and wanted the King's power for himself. He challenged the King and the King gave him over to his wicked ways. Now he can never come into the Kingdom again and he's jealous because he knows we can go home but he's stuck here forever."

"The King will forgive us for wrongs we do if we ask forgiveness. We can prevent transgressions of the Kingdom Rules by learning his decrees. The King's thoughts are in his words and when we earnestly study his instructions; his thoughts are revealed to us. Doesn't that make you feel good to know that the King not only loves you, but he trust you with his thoughts. Lucre can never be trusted."

"Lucre can never call the King's Kingdom his home again. Someday I will tell you the whole story, but today we must be about our work. Don't worry Gayla the King will save us because he loves us. He loves all he created, but not all will love him. All who agree to live in love can be His children. The one who made himself an enemy of the King has rejected love. Lucre and all those who would side against the King desired power over love."

At that moment rushing out of the shadows, two goons seized Christian, one on either side of him. The evil beings bound Christian tightly with the rope carried on their belts. When he was bound the men turned him around and there stood Lucre. It had been a long time since Christian stood face to face with Lucre. Lucre had stayed a distance from the boy.

Now looking into the boy's eyes he saw a similarity of the King. Lucre stepped back slightly. To steady his heart beat, Christian was softly repeating the King's promise under his breath, "No weapon formed against me shall ever prosper." But even softly, the words rang true. Lucre heard the truth and again he stepped further away from the boy.

Speaking to the leader of his vile gang, he instructed him "Hold him until the party is in full swing and everyone is inebriated." Christian looked directly at Lucre as he was walking away. Lucre's form became part of the shadows. Lucre was one with the darkness.

The party had been under way for hours now. It was now the midnight hour and it seemed as if all the children both young and old were completely drunk under Lucre's intoxicating formula. The drink seem to weave a spell over the children. There was all manner of evil taking place. Men were fighting among themselves, women were using foul language, and all the children had given themselves over to Lucre's evil.

Lucre stood and surveyed the chaos about him. He felt pleased with himself. But once again he underestimated the King's love for the children. Not having love, Lucre could never fathom how strong love could be. So he proceeded to plan how the children would help him to hurt the King never considering the power of love to overcome evil.

They had been little help to him in building his Kingdom, but tonight they would help him and seal their own fate. Lucre felt sure the King would be too angry not to punish the children once they burned that little troublemaker at the stake. "No, I can't hurt him directly, but a little seductive coaching will get these drunken idiots to carry out my scheme. They all have a price. A little comfort and they turn on each other," Lucre told the goon beside him. Lucre would never understand how strong the King's love is.

Not understanding the King's love, did not prevent him knowing that the King expected all the children to love each other. Knowing he could not directly touch the children, he was a master at using the children's thoughts to prevail over their natural inclination to love.

Lucre had taught his followers to shoot fiery darts into the minds of the children. These darts were unseen and could be felt only after their poison was emptied into the thoughts of the children. The darts consisted of all manner of evil possibilities for the children. The darts carried the power of suggestion into the thoughts of the children and the thought became a seed planted into their hearts.

Lucre would suggest dreadful things into the children's thoughts by whispering into their ear until the child's mind accepted the suggestion as truth. At that point the suggestion became a reality to the child. Sometimes the darts held the poison of jealousy, selfishness, even hatred. The poison combined with the power of suggestion had caused many children to faint and grow weak. Some even fell into the sleep of death.

Lucre had many vials of poison to use against the children. He took great joy in using the poison of sickness. He enjoyed this one because the uninformed children didn't know that sickness could not live in their bodies unless they nurtured it.

It amazed him how quickly the children would take possession of the suggestion. After accepting the suggestion, the children would allow the sickness to control their thoughts. At that point the heart accepted the sickness and it manifested itself within their earth bodies, taking control as well. When he had convinced them to accept such things his work was complete because they would do the rest. That's what he was planning for tonight.

Tonight he would convince the children to do something so bad the King would have to show his anger toward them or so he thought. Tonight he would whisper lies about Christian and Gayla until the other children were driven to hurt the two. The King wanted the children to live in love and tonight he would use that desire of the King to destroy them and get even with the King.

It was late into the night and there were fights breaking out among the drunken children. After years of hard work the children went wild with the chance to have unrestricted fun. With no supervision and no one to tell them what to do, they were out of control. The desire of their earth bodies completely overruled the spirit within. Lucre was very please to see every one so aggravated. Lucre thought to himself, "I will make more parties like this. Of course I'll have to steal more children because at this rate it won't be long before they all kill each other. They're easy to replace."

Lucre knew he had no real powers, but he could use his lies to trick the unsatisfied children into using the power the King gave them to hurt each other. But first he would have to get Christian and anyone like him out of the way. "So long as there are children like Christian around, the King's decrees will continue to be taught and spread to others. Not even my most convincing magic can stop the truth when spoken by the King's children. Just as hearing my lies builds confidence in them, so does hearing the truth build confidence in them. This spoken word stuff is so powerful. The only way I can win is to shut the truth up and continue to speak my lies. Once that boy and any other believers are out of the way, the truth should be shut up. Then I can have it my way."

Lucre knew he could not win; he was only lying to himself. Lucre was an example of what can happen when we don't live by the truth. If you live only by lies, it becomes hard to know the difference between lies and truth. But truth always wins.

The drunken rivalry continued on through the night and well into the next day. Many were injured while committing acts they had never dreamed of before this party. The children lay on the ground all over the campsite. The new clothes were torn and covered with black ashen dirt. No one would ever think the clothes were new. Like everything given by Lucre, they didn't last for long. No gift given by Lucre can last, because like Lucre, his gifts are fleeting.

At noon, Lucre signaled his gang to get the children on their feet. The children were made to stand in their sleepy state. Being condition to work, most thought it was time to go back to work. The children had changed. Not only were they half asleep, there was a cloud of darkness about them. Katerboro was always gloomy, but this darkness was attached directly to the children. The darkness prevented the children seeing clearly.

The children could not see their changes, but they felt different. They felt more hopeless than ever. Lucre's gang was able to lead the children into the pit at the camp without any resistance. Once the children realized they were not being summoned for work, they went happily. Like sheep being led to a slaughter, the children were led into the pit that Lucre's gang had made ready before the party.

Lucre stood up on the highest point in the ash-covered camp, about fifteen feet in front of the pit and raised his bony arms with crooked fingers pointing in the air. With arms raised he looked all around, first to one side then to the other side for great effect. Lucre began to speak. "There are those among you that would fill your minds with dreams of a King who loves you. He is a King that will take you to a beautiful place and give you all that you need. Look at yourselves. Do you really believe that a great, fine King could love you? You are filthy, dirty and destroying each other. Why would a good King love you? You desired good things and I gave them to you only yesterday. Now today they are torn and ragged, because you are who you are. You are not children of a King. A King's children would be good and clean, not filthy and evil like you. That's why the King sent you here to this place. You think I brought you here, but if he is great he could have saved you, if he wanted too. But he allowed you to come here because you are bad."

Hearing the lie, the children looked around at the surroundings. Although it was now after noon, there was no sun. There was never any sun in this place. Yet the heat was always hot. Steam rose out of the cracks in the dry ground. If there was a Great King that loved them like Christian said, why didn't he rescue them from this awful place? Hearing the lie of Lucre, the children accepted it as truth.

Lucre continued to speak, "It's time you face the truth and know that no King can love unclean children like you. Need I remind you of the acts you committed yesterday? Who taught you those filthy deeds? It's on the inside of you. Don't let anyone trick you. In fact you should be angry with those who tried to fool you. They are only laughing at you. This is the only place where you can stay."

The children began to see themselves as Lucre said they were. They began to feel anger at Christian for trying to give them hope when there was no hope. Looking around at all the destruction they caused, they felt they were not fit to live in a Kingdom. They were only good enough for this dirty place.

Lucre felt that he was gaining ground, convincing the children to think his way. Soften his tone and he spoke as though he cared. "You have to depend on yourselves. Don't trust the one on your left or the one on your right. Look at the scars you have from one night. If I left you by yourself for a week, what would you do to each other? I watch out over you. I care for you because you have no one else."

Lucre stopped for a minute to allow what he had said to sink into the children's minds. The children were eyeing each other with distrust. Many withdrew to stand alone. Others began to circle around one another remembering hurtful words spoken yesterday. It was as though at any moment they would begin to fight again. Lucre felt that now was the time to strike.

"Where is this Christian, the one who talks of his Father's love? Why is he not here among his brothers and sisters? I'll tell you why. Because he feels that he is above you. He feels he is not dirty like you. Isn't he always telling you to change? What makes him better than you? When you make mistakes his kind will never stand with you. His kind will always look down on you. Do you know why? To live in their precious Kingdom, you have to be perfect. Is there any among you that feel like you can become perfect? Of course not. What chance could you possible have?"

A low mumble started in the crowd and everyone looked around for Christian. The mummer grew louder, "Where is Christian?" Suddenly the guilt they were feeling toward themselves was being directed at Christian. After all he was no better than they were. "Why hadn't he joined the party? They had never been good enough for him, with all his lofty ideas of his Father, the King."

Lucre felt certain that things were working the way he wanted. "The silly children are so easy to deceive. They are always so uncertain, never believing. With doubt and guilt he was able to sway these silly children every time it seems. Now to get rid of that Christian and he could be about his business. Hadn't Christian already infected that silly girl, Gayla? No more, he would put a stop to it."

But there was one among the crowd looking for Christian for a different reason. The one called Jason. Like Gayla he had heard the truth in the words spoken by Christian. In a dream the Kingdom of the King had appeared in all its' splendor to Jason. Jason longed to see the reality of such a place for himself. For this reason he had sought the King and been rewarded with hearing the King speak to him.

Jason had spent continuous time in speaking to the unseen King on behalf of Gayla. He did not ask the King to whisk him away to the beautiful Kingdom, he ask the King to save Gayla. For this reason the King was pleased with Jason and because of the time spent with the King, Jason knew something was happening tonight. Eyes wide open and listening to the crowd, Jason was ready.

During the night Christian had asked Gayla to join him in talking to the King. At first Gayla felt odd talking to someone she couldn't see with her eyes while Christian was there with her. Oh yes she felt him, but it seemed odd to speak to the unseen King while Christian was near. Christian sensed that although she believed, Gayla felt odd so he spoke to her. "Gayla if you will let your heart speak, soon the words will flow from your mouth. Trust Gala, that's the key, just trust and surrender." So Gayla started to speak as though the King was right before her. It felt good to be able to tell all her thoughts, all her sadness and worries to someone else. Speaking gave her freedom to admit her fears and to ask for strength and courage. Soon she forgot Christian was there.

Once she began talking, the pain and sorrow became more than she could bear and the tears flowed like water. She could hear Christian speaking also, but it was as though no one was there except a strange comforting presence that gave her peace. Christian hearing the pain in the young girl's voice began to cry softly. It was too dark for either of them to see the other's face, but they each felt the presence of the King.

Anger rose up in Christian toward Lucre for what he was doing to the children. Christian's heart reminded the King of his promise to deliver all that would believe. Christian spoke to the King on behalf of the other children. Lucre had tricked the children into coming here, but the unknown child had made sure they would never have to stay here. Christian wanted Lucre to be defeated in his own backyard.

Christian and Gayla talked to the King until they were exhausted, but not tired. As they talked, peace came into their hearts and with the peace came strength. So they were not tired, just empty and with that they feel asleep. They were at peace.

Meanwhile Lucre was busy beguiling the children. "Listen, let's start the party back. Why get down about a King that doesn't exist and if he does, he doesn't care about you. Let's eat, drink and be merry." The children were slow to start moving, but gradually they lifted the poison ale Lucre had supplied. Taking long swallows they were soon dancing and laughing again. But for more than one child, the laughter was mixed with tears. Yet for a little while they could forget their pain and pretend they were free.

The children were completely under Lucre's control, believing that this life was all they would ever have. They were like starving children who really wanted chocolate cake but only had green peas to eat, so rather than starve they held onto the green peas. The poor children wanted so much more, but they found it hard to believe there was more. Lucre knew this and he used the children's doubt to help his evil plans.

By now they were fighting and causing pain to one another again. After Lucre's talk they felt even more unworthy and beat at each other as if to beat the images created by Lucre's words from their minds. They were more reckless than before. Scratching and clawing they were intent on inflicting hurt. Lucre knew it was time to move into the final stage of his plan to get rid of Christian and Gayla. Lucre had decided the best way to get rid of the children, was to let them destroy each other including Christian and Gayla.

"Yes," Lucre thought, "just a while longer and they would be ready to destroy that meddlesome boy. This boy dared to interfere with him in his desires to control the children. What a silly boy, did he think he could fight him and win?" But once again Lucre did not understand the King or his ways. Lucre was always blind when it came to the King.

The King never intended his children to stand-alone against Lucre. What he wanted was for his children to accept his word and to have conviction in his promises. He wanted them to know every word was true. The King wanted his children to have enough confidence to declare the truth of His words even in the face of death. To love life more than the one who gives life would be foolish. When the children put the King before all else, he would never let them down. When Lucre touched the children he became an enemy of the Kingdom. The King had issued a proclamation of war on all evil!

However not believing or knowing these things, the children continued doing what Lucre expected. They were fighting, drinking and using words that should never be spoken. Evil deposits were left by these words long after they had been spoken. Bad words they learned from Lucre's gang.

Lucre was happy, thinking that winning was all about who had the best tricks. When Lucre felt that he had fully convinced the children to think his way, he signaled for Christian and Gayla to be brought into the area.

The children were still inside the pit but immediately Jason spotted the pair. Lucre had Christian and Gayla place on a high hill. Hands tied behind their backs, Christian and Gayla could see what a mess the other children were in.

Lucre's men grabbed the hands of both of the children and stretched their arms high above their heads. The arms of both children were tied very tight to a limb hanging from an angry black tree. Christian spoke aloud so Gayla would hear him, "We have more freedom here than those in that pit." The fiends howled with laughter, not understanding what was meant by the words. They thought the children were gone mad. Christian knew that all the ropes in the world could not bind his Father and he knew no ropes would take away the freedom provided by the sacrifice of the unknown child.

By now the children were aware that Christian and Gayla had been brought upon the hill. Lucre spoke and the children listened as though they under his spell. "Here are the great believers. The ones who were going to lead you to the King's great Kingdom. Look at yourselves. You are covered in mud, blood and dirt. These two are not one of you. They don't share your pain or your fun. They place themselves above you. They want to be better than you. See how clean they are?"

Turing to the fiend nearest him Lucre spoke in a low voice, "Why are they clean?" The great goon shrugged his shoulders and Lucre continued on through somewhat puzzled.

"When we caught them they were laughing at you. They called you stupid. Do you really think they would take you with them if they run away? Wake up and see this is the only home you'll ever have. Where else can you go? Don't let them make you unhappy with what you have. Their aim is to control your mind."

The crowds began to mummer and agree with what Lucre was speaking. Inside the children knew the words were not true but it was easier to agree and to feel accepted, than to challenge the lies and risk Lucre's anger. "Besides Christian did act like he was from a different world and he was always bragging about his Father, the King. So maybe he was laughing at them, who could tell? And now look at Gayla. Here all this time they thought she was being held by Lucre and now she turns up with Christian. She couldn't be trusted. Before she started hanging with Christian, she was one of them."

Now that Lucre had the crowd warmed up, he suggested a test. "If his Father is really a King, let's test him. After all a King would be able to save him and her right?" At this point many in the crowd began to feel uneasy. They felt something was happening but they didn't really want to be part of whatever it was. But many others jeered and shouted in agreement with Lucre. These same children were agreeing with Lucre to test the truth about the King.

Now Lucre knew it was very dangerous to make the King angry, but he was hiding behind the children. Lucre spoke, "Let's build a fire at the bottom of this hill. It will take several hours for the flame to reach the top of the mountain. If this King is real, surely he will save them before the fire consumes them"

"No!" came a scream from the back of the pit. One of the elders had screamed the word. The woman was older than some of the others, so she remembered a little about the King. This woman had been one of the first to run away when the unknown child was killed. Suddenly the horror of that night flashed into her mind and she was terrified. Her fear had made her run from the King's love before tasting his forgiveness. In her heart how she longed for a second chance, maybe this was her second chance. "It is written we must not test the King," she said. The words long forgotten came from teachings of long ago.

When Lucre heard these words he turned all green and yellow with envy for the King. The woman had been here for many years, yet the words of the King were still with her. "So there were other believers here also," he thought. "They must be wiped out. But first, let's get rid of this boy." He sent his men to mingle with the crowd and encourage the children that the test should be performed."

Standing outside the group and watching, Jason felt someone touch his shoulder. There beside him stood a figure dressed in a white robe. The figure was clearly out of place among the dark dingy surroundings but no one seems to notice it. Jason did not know the figure could only be seen by him. The figure motioned Jason behind a rock face. There piled high was the most magnificent battle armor Jason had ever seen.

"Jason you have been chosen to do the work of the King along with your brother Christian," the figure in the white robe spoke. "Wait here and the King will cause others to come to you. Because of your belief take the robe of virtue woven from the blood of the unknown child and wear it forever. As others join you they too shall receive their own robe."

At the top of the hill Christian raised his voice to speak. "My Father has said that his children know his voice and they will not listen to the voice of evil. Will you choose to be children of a King or would you prefer to live among the pigs forever? The choice is yours."

"Proclaim with your voice that he is King and you want the Royal garment woven of the blood of the unknown child. Ask the King to give it to you and he will." At the mention of the unknown child Lucre cringed with rage. Christian continued on, "Testify to the sovereignty of the King and receive wisdom. Wisdom is your protection from lies. That which is borne of a lie will fade. It doesn't matter if it's a friendship or a gift, it will fade. Look it your new clothes, they look old after only one day. It's because a lie can never last and whatever comes from a lie will fade away."

Gayla called out, "Listen to Christian he speaks truth." For some of the children the fog inside their heads began to clear and they could discern the truth of Christian's words. "After all Gayla was one of them, she too had suffered day and night in this place. What could she gain by lying?"

These began to feel shame for their actions. They began to see that in the past they were living as they were forced to, but over the last twenty-four hours, they were living as they decided to. No one made them drink the foul liquid or fight their brothers and sisters. They were acting out of choice. Yes they desired wisdom. At that moment they realized even though they lived in a place they did not desire, they could choose to hope for a better life. "What was the word Christian used? There was a word he used," the crowd began to ask. Then someone remembered and said,

"**Faith**." Hearing the word, the crowd picked it up and one by one they each spoke the word. The meaning of the word deepens each time it was repeated.

The children did not realize that it was the King's spirit that was speaking to them. They had no knowledge of the King so they did not recognize him when they heard him, but Jason knew. While speaking to the children the Spirit of the King was guiding the believers back to where Jason stood. Upon arrival many were ashamed, but all ask for the garment woven in the blood of the unknown child. Quietly Jason took the believer to the back of the rock face and instructed him how the battle armor was worn.

Each child accepted the garment woven of the unknown child's blood from the figure in white before putting on the battle armor. Proclaiming their faith in the King to save them entitled them to be pardon of all wrong choices of the past. The figure in the white robe declared each "Not guilty" and wrote their names in the book he carried.

Lucre though not aware of Jason and the children behind the rock face, felt he was losing control and he began to look around for someone that was still under his spell. Lucre scanned the crowd and his eyes fell on Samuel and Chen. Quickly he sent one of his gang over to the two boys. As always he put a challenge to the boys. Chen not knowing it is better to enter into the King's rest rather than face temptation was easy prey for what was coming. The King wants His children to let him take care of them. Then there is no need to respond to every challenge put before them, but Chen didn't know this because he didn't believe.

Lucre's goons ask the boys, "Why not set the fire and see if the King comes, then we will all know the truth." Just as before the goons had limited knowledge of the King's determination to save his children. The clean up boys overheard the challenge and looking at Chen ask, "Ready for your induction in the gang?" The group was ever seeking to please Lucre. They enjoyed the status obeying Lucre seem to give them. Samuel turned to Chen, "What say we prove him?" Chen hesitated for a moment, and then gave way to the temptation to be part of the group. He wanted to belong.

Although the thought was planted by Lucre, at that moment Samuel gave way to his own evil desire to set the fire and only the grace of the King could cleanse him. But to get the King's grace he would have to realize what he did and ask for forgiveness. Samuel was blind to truth and did not see the evil behind his deed.

Chen and the others picked up torches and followed Samuel over to the hill where the two children were tied. Looking around they were careful to see that no one saw them, but Lucre watched in eager anticipation. There was another who saw them also. There was one who watched in sorrow to see His children led on a path of destruction and pain.

Lucre of course was delighted he had found someone to carry out his wicked plan. Lucre knew that as much he hated the children, he could not accomplish his evil deeds without them.

His greediness to be a King had left him with nothing. Lucre tried to convince himself he could control the children. Again this was one of his lies. Lucre could not control the children. All it took for the children to be free was acceptance of the King. They knew the goodness of the King inside their heart, but they had to choose it. They simply needed to believe in the King and to chose love over evil to lose Lucre's hold over their lives.

So watching Chen, Samuel and the others rush toward the two on the hill, Lucre lied to himself that he was in charge. He tried to convince himself that perhaps he could destroy even if he couldn't create. This too was a lie. Lucre can cause hurt only if he is believed.

Poor Chen and the others had no idea of Lucre's thoughts as they ran toward the hill with the lighted torches. Here they were running blindly into danger to satisfy the desire of Lucre. Their minds blinded to all attempts to enlighten them to their identity. Using their will they carried out the plan of someone who did not have a choice. When Lucre was kicked out of the Kingdom; all choice was taken from him. He would be evil without recourse just as he intended the children to be. However because of the unknown child, the children had a choice.

While Chen and the others were carrying out their foolish deed, many in the crowd began to see Lucre as the liar he really was. All the while Christian and Gayla had not stopped talking to the King. As they talked they petition the King to show the truth to the other children. Not all would receive the truth as it entered their heart, but to those desiring truth, slowly the truth was becoming clearer. These through design began to walk toward the rock where Jason stood.

Then Christian began to speak to the crowd as the King gave him the words. His words sounded loud and strong over the desolate enclave. "When you have done this deed, you will not be heroes. You will have accomplished what Lucre wants and when you fulfill his desire to control you, he will push you to destroy yourself. Lucre can't help you here or anywhere else. He has no power. He needs you to help him! He can't free you because he has no freedom. He's trapped here until the King destroys him for good. Don't be swayed to believe his lies. Do not be afraid. No weapon formed against you can succeed. The unknown child has given us power over all the entrapments and lies of the evil one. Because of the blood sacrifice paid by the unknown child, nothing can hurt you if you will just accept the price paid and speak your acceptance with your mouth. Swear allegiance to the King and allow him to save you."

The Children were still dazed and confused from Lucre's spell. In addition they were afraid because they didn't know the King. Jason and the children who had chosen to adorn the battle armor for the Kingdom were busy readying themselves for war. This included given thankful testimony in appreciation of the sacrifice of the unknown child as they swore allegiance to the King. Each child was told to depend on the King by speaking His words in the battle. The King's Spirit would empower the words to complete the task they were spoken for.

The children knew only enough to know they desired a changed and to believe that this garment would give them the change they needed. "Speak the word of the King that you do know and He will give you more," they were told. "Even if you only know one word of the King, it has more power than all the powers of evil here or anywhere else." They had enough knowledge for the King to free them. They would grow in knowledge as they spent time with the King in talking to him. This was their starting point, a new beginning.

Lucre unaware the children were donning the garments woven of the blood from the unknown child waited in anticipation for the Chen and the cleanup boys to make their next move. Suddenly the ground was littered with the huge ugly birds that came when a dead carcass was on the ground. The birds were giant size and ghastly to behold. The enclave was covered with them.

The children were looking at the birds and wondering why they were here. Lucre had not summoned the birds and they wondered who did. Normally the children took cover when the birds appeared but there was no where to hide out in the enclave. The birds were large enough to left a large hog off the ground and fly away with it. It was never safe to turn your back on these birds. They might carry live things away if they were really hungry. The birds came in anticipation of dead meat.

The children receiving the special garments had become instruments of joy. The same joy the King had used to cement the foundation of love in the beginning. This joy brought strength to the children. These children could be heard singing, the birds were of no threat to them. Standing at the top of the hill, Christian and Gayla looked at the huge birds. The wind rose and lashed out at the two. Gales tore at the children's cheeks and threaten to tear their arms from the shoulder. The nor'easter whipped the black ashen dirt into a small whirlwind around them. Both Christian and Gayla knew rescue was imminent. Several of the birds circled above the two. The pair was not disturbed. There was a clam peacefulness imbedded deep within them. There was a sureness of victory and they too began to sing with joy. Nothing could take their joy, not even the huge ugly birds.

Many did not receive joy because they had hardened their hearts against the truth and refuse to believe. As much as He wanted to help; without belief it was impossible for the King to help them. The unbelieving children would not ask the King for help. Lost and without direction and they stumbled around the enclave in darkness. Stubborn refusing to believe they did not know which way to turn for help.

As if in response to the singing, five beautiful white birds flew from the eastern sky. Unlike the loud squawking coming from the huge ugly birds, these were cooing and singing along with the children. They created more beauty than any had ever seen in Katerboro. Lucre bristled at the sight. How he long to have such beauty attributed to his name. Jealousy raged inside him. "Set the blasted fire" he called out to no one in particular.

The children for once were not listening to Lucre. The beautiful sound of the birds bought comfort to the children. None of the children had ever seen such beautiful birds. The five birds circled around and round overhead before landing on Christian and Gayla. With the arrival of the beautiful white birds, the huge ugly birds retreated a distance away. From the distance they gawked and stared, but did not come closer. Then as though summoned by some unknown voice, the beautiful white birds flew swiftly away. Just as suddenly as they came, they were gone.

In the next instant the hill became a blazing inferno. Samuel and the other boys had reached their goal and put the torches to the hill. Chen stood frozen, his torch still in his hand. One of the clean up crew struck him across the mouth and snatching the torch threw it onto the burning hill. Chen fell to the ground and threw up.

Screams were heard from the pit. Confused children felt as though they were in a nightmare. The bright flames illuminated the pit and ghostly shadows danced around. Even some of the children filled with joy were becoming anxious. They took strength by encouraging each other. One day they would have strength to stand alone, but for today's ordeal they needed each other. There was confusion everywhere.

Quickly Jason urged those with him into battle. The white birds were the sign for the warriors of the Kingdom to come forth. Taken by surprise Lucre had never expected the armed children who suddenly appeared. Armed in Royal armor the children were an impressive sight. Carrying shields coated in faith and swords dipped in truth the army of children radiated confidence. Lucre's goons were never equipped when confronted with the truth of the Kingdom. The children rushed toward the goons with swords raised speaking words of victory. "Die you evil demons," they yelled.

Trying to muster a defense against the Royal children the goons were quickly losing ground. The battle raged as the goons attacked with threw fiery darts thrown at the children. Only the children without armor were wounded. However the longer the children stood their ground, the smaller the darts became. As the battle continued to rage soon there was shift in the fighting; no longer were the children under attack, but the children became the attackers. The children dressed in the Royal armor stood firmly in the special shoes provided for them. Each time the arrows of the goons were deflected the confidence of the children grew. With the growing confidence they gained strength. The strength in turn built up joy within the children. The joy of the King was evident in the children even in the heat of the battle. No longer timid, the joyous children rushed to destroy their enemies. High above and out of sight, the King and the unknown child smiled on the beloved children.

The battle went on for what seemed like hours. Tired and seeing the children standing firm, Jason put his shield down for a moment. Immediately a fiery dart fired by Lucre landed on the boy. Lucre was waiting for someone to drop their shield. The boy began to fall. From across the yard, Chen was watching the bravery of the newly transformed children. Seeing Jason began to fall Chen ran toward the falling boy. Chen's heart had heard the call of the King.

Picking up a sword he rushed to the aide of the fallen boy. Shouting words of the King he remembered from Christian, Chen stood over Jason and pulled the fiery dart loose. Jason lying on the ground heard the words and received power from them. But Chen had entered the battle without the proper armor and just as Jason lifted his shield to fight once more, Chen was mortally wounded by one of Lucre's goons.

Chen lay at Jason's feet with his life force leaving his body as the blood drained from the wound. Kneeling Jason covered the wounded boy with his shield and began administrating the truth of the King's spoken power to the wound. "Chen do you accept the garment woven of blood by the unknown child?" No one could wear the garment unless they ask for it. Because of his change of heart, Chen was able to answer "Yes, give it to me." Out of no where the figure in the white robe appeared with the blood garment in hand and placed it on the bleeding boy. "Chen listen to me. You are innocent because of the unknown child. Death has no right to you. Do understand what I'm saying to you? Fight this Chen. Do not accept that which is not yours. You have the right to life." Jason kept his shield of faith over the weak boy until the figure in the white garment provided Chen with his own shield. The shield began to strengthen as Chen accepted the promises of the King. The blood garment was replacing the blood which had oozed from the boy and the life force of the King restored life into the dying boy. Strengthen with new life; the two beat back the fangs of death using the King's words to declare victory.

All this time the fire had been creeping up the hill toward the now forgotten boy and girl tied at the top. Without any warning water in the form of rain began to fall from the sky. Never had the children seen this happen before.

As the water fell, the truth began to divide the children. The unbelievers were now on one side and the believing children were on the other side.

Without knowing how it happen, the children had been moved to a place the King choose for them. Everything from the past was being washed away from the believing children. They were clean.

Stunned the unbelievers realized the water from the sky was not falling on them, only on the believers. The dirt was being washed from the believers and they were becoming clean, while the unbelievers remained dirty. Some of the unbelievers tried to move over to the other side but it was as though an invisible wall separated the two teams.

By the time the water fell, the fire had reached Christian and Gayla. The flames totally engulfed the two children, they were no where to be seen. The astonished children froze looking at the hill. Faces shining and eyes reflecting the victory of the battle, they stood looking at fire where once Christian and Gayla had stood. Just as the water stopped, Christian and Gayla walked out of the flames unharmed. It was only then the flames went out. Christian and Gayla ran down the hill holding hands and shouting joyful noises to the King. Cheers rose from the victorious children.

With all the noise in the camp, at first no one heard the rumble coming up from the depths of the earth. That is no one but Lucre. Lucre and his dirty little band was separated from both the believing children and the unbelieving children. Added to the rumble in the ground there came a rumbling from the sky. And as strange as it may seem, the believing children instead of feeling fear were overcome with joy. So much that they began to dance and shout. The shouts were sounds of victory!

When Christian had reached the bottom of the hill, the first person he grabbed was Chen. Chen was on the side of the believers. The two boys hugged each other and shouted the sound of victory and freedom. Chen was crying and repeating how sorry he was for what he had done. Chen said he was sorry for not believing. At that moment Chen heard a still quite voice coming from inside his heart. The voice said, "You are forgiven" and Chen felt peace for the first time in his life.

Christian told Chen to hurry and help him get the believing children together. The King was telling Christian to move the children toward the light in the center in the big mountain on the east. Jason and all the children covered in the blood garment, quickly assembled and began to move the way Christian indicated. Shouts of victory were coming from the children. As they approached the mountain, the light coming from inside grew brighter.

A hand covered in brilliant sparkling light reached down from the sky stretching the opening in the mountain until the light was big enough for all the children to pass through.

Cries of despair could be heard coming from the unbelieving children left behind them. Christian without turning to look told everyone to keep moving forward and not to look back. All the children pass through the opening.

Fire began to fall down on the side they had come from and the huge ugly birds could be heard making eating sounds. The believing children began to cry softly, but obeying they never turned around. One girl asks, "Will they ever get out?" Christian answered, "Just believe and trust the King. All things are possible to those who believe."

Gayla, Chen and Jason marched at the front of the line with Christian. Jason ask Christian how long would it be before they reached the Kingdom. Now that the battle was over he long to see the place he had dreamed of. Just then a voice from the heavens was heard and the sky became a beautiful blue for the first time they could remember.

The voice said, "The Kingdom is always with you when you obey. The beauty of the Kingdom is your peace. The joy you received today is a reward of the Kingdom."

THE END

Printed in the United States
By Bookmasters